HARCOURT SCHOOL PUBLISHERS

Think Math!

Spiral Review Book

Developed by Education Development Center, Inc. through National Science Foundation
Grant No. ESI-0099093
EDC

Harcourt
SCHOOL PUBLISHERS

Visit *The Learning Site!*
www.harcourtschool.com/thinkmath

HARCOURT SCHOOL PUBLISHERS

Think Math!

Printed in the United States of America

ISBN 13: 978-0-15-342491-5

ISBN 10: 0-15-342491-5

1 2 3 4 5 6 7 8 9 10 170 16 15 14 13 12 11 10 09 08 07

This program was funded in part through the National Science Foundation under Grant No. ESI-0099093. Any opinions, findings, and conclusions or recommendations expressed in this program are those of the authors and do not necessarily reflect the views of the National Science Foundation.

Think Math! # Contents

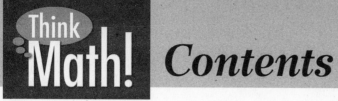

Think Math!

Contents

Chapter 5 Area and Perimeter

Chapter 6 Multi-Digit Multiplication

Chapter 7 Fractions

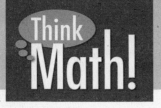

Chapter 8 Decimals

Chapter 9 Measurement

Chapter 10 Data and Probability

Chapter 11 Three-Dimensional Geometry

Think Math! **Contents**

These pages provide review of previously learned skills and concepts. The Spiral Review Book pages provide a comprehensive overview of math skills taught in the program.

Spiral Review Book

Name ______________________ Date ____________

Spiral Review
Lesson 1

Number and Operations

Find the difference.

1. 361 − 174 = ☐	2. 402 − 226 = ☐	3. 554 − 108 = ☐	4. 1,325 − 1,018 = ☐
5. 2,108 − 1,593 = ☐	6. 793 − 607 = ☐	7. 914 − 492 = ☐	8. 2,668 − 1,812 = ☐
9. 6,219 − 5,185 = ☐	10. 7,931 − 5,893 = ☐	11. 1,004 − 587 = ☐	12. 5,030 − 2,681 = ☐

13. 800 − 219 = ______

14. 9,005 − 7,672 = ______

Measurement

Use the starting time and the time interval to find the ending time.

15. Start doing homework at 4:00 P.M. Work for 1 hour 15 minutes.

______

16. Start walking to school at 7:50 A.M. Walk for 25 minutes.

______

17. Start playing basketball at 3:55 P.M. Play for 1 hour 30 minutes.

______

18. Start trip to grandmother's house at 8:10 A.M. Travel for 2 hours 45 minutes.

______

19. Start working in the garden at 10:35 A.M. Work for 3 hours 10 minutes.

______

20. Start walking home from school at 3:55 P.M. Walk for 22 minutes.

______

Name ______________________ Date ______________

Spiral Review
Lesson 2

Geometry

Write the number of pairs of parallel sides and the number of right angles.

1.

Pairs of parallel sides ☐

Right angles ☐

2.
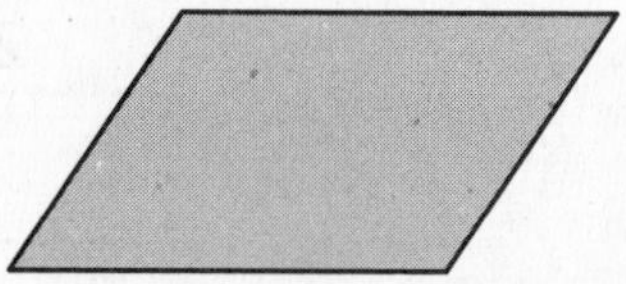

Pairs of parallel sides ☐

Right angles ☐

3.
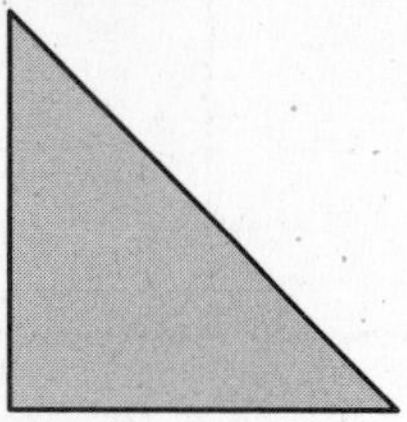

Pairs of parallel sides ☐

Right angles ☐

4.
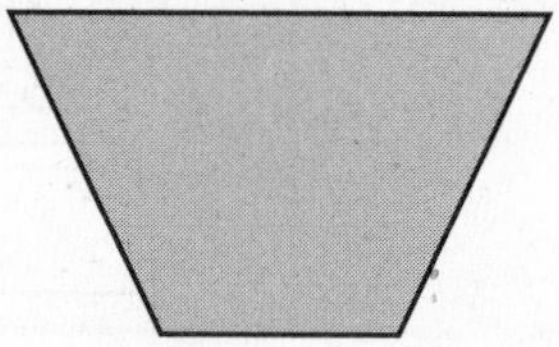

Pairs of parallel sides ☐

Right angles ☐

Problem Solving

Solve the problem. Explain your answer.

5. Ryan gets on the elevator at the ground floor, which is numbered 0. He rides up 7 floors, down 3, up 2, down 1, and, up 5. On which floor does he get off the elevator? ☐

____

____

____

____

____

____

____

Name ______________________ Date ______________

Spiral Review
Lesson 3

Number and Operations

Write multiplication and division fact families for each set of numbers.

1. 7, 2, 14

____

____

2. 8, 5, 40

____

____

3. 5, 5, 25

____

____

4. 9, 7, 63

____

____

5. 3, 7, 21

____

____

6. 6, 9, 54

____

____

Data Analysis and Probability

For 7–9, use the pictograph.

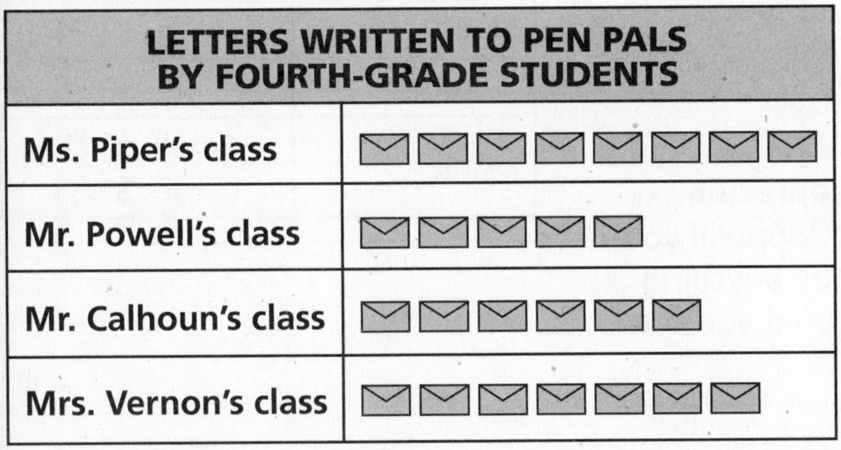

Key: Each  **= 5 letters.**

7. Were there *more than* or *less than* 100 letters written in all?

____

8. How many more letters did Ms. Piper's class write than Mr. Powell's class?

____

9. Which two classes together wrote exactly 60 letters?

____

Name ______________________ Date ____________

Measurement

Write the equivalent measure.

1. 1 pound = [16] ounces	2. 32 ounces = [ ] pounds
3. 1 ton = [2,000] pounds	4. 4,000 pounds = [ ] tons
5. 3 pounds = [ ] ounces	6. 2 tons = [ ] pounds
7. 64 ounces = [ ] pounds	8. 5 tons = [ ] pounds
9. 1,000 pounds = [ ] ton	10. 5 pounds = [ ] ounces
11. $\frac{1}{2}$ pound = [ ] ounces	12. 24 ounces = [ ] pounds

Reasoning and Proof

For 13–15, use the price chart.

Item	Price
Sandwich	$3.95
Salad	$2.95
Side dish	$0.75
Drink	Small: $1.15 Large: $1.55

13. What is the greatest number of sandwiches you can buy, and spend less than $15?

____

14. If you buy the greatest possible number of sandwiches for less than $15, will you have enough left over to buy anything else on the menu? If so, what could you buy?

____

15. You have $10. If you buy at least one sandwich, what else could you buy in order to spend as much of your money as possible but not more than $10?

____

Name ______________________ Date ______________

Spiral Review
Lesson 5

Number and Operations

Find the quotient.

1 $5\overline{)30}$	2 $9\overline{)27}$	3 $2\overline{)14}$	4 $6\overline{)42}$
5 $8\overline{)72}$	6 $3\overline{)15}$	7 $4\overline{)36}$	8 $12\overline{)60}$
9 $3\overline{)24}$	10 $8\overline{)64}$	11 $7\overline{)56}$	12 $11\overline{)55}$
13 $10\overline{)90}$	14 $4\overline{)16}$	15 $7\overline{)49}$	16 $5\overline{)45}$
17 $11\overline{)88}$	18 $6\overline{)54}$	19 $8\overline{)32}$	20 $12\overline{)96}$

Geometry

Circle each prism and mark an "X" over each pyramid.

21

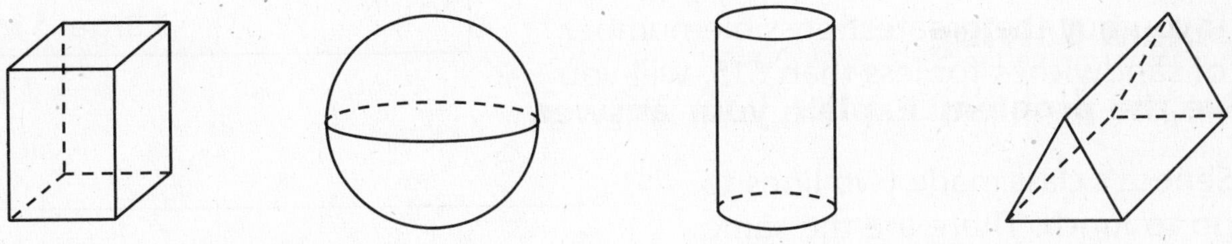

22

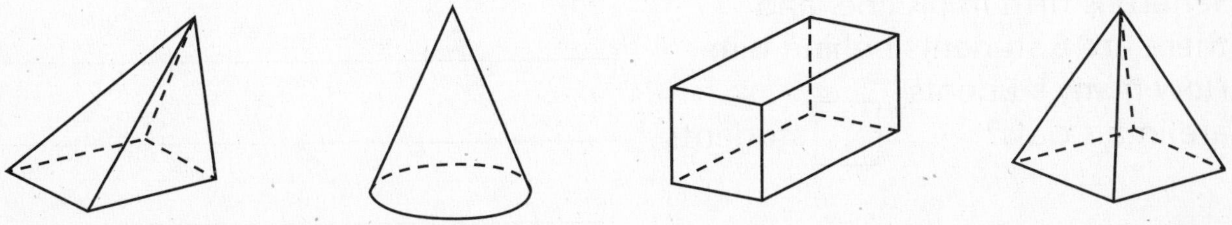

Name ______________________ Date ______________

Algebra

Use a pattern to complete each multiplication set.

1 $2 \times 8 =$ ____ $20 \times 8 =$ ____ $200 \times 8 =$ ____	2 $3 \times 5 =$ ____ $30 \times 5 =$ ____ $300 \times 5 =$ ____	3 $4 \times 8 =$ ____ $4 \times 80 =$ ____ $4 \times 800 =$ ____
4 $9 \times 2 =$ ____ $9 \times 20 =$ ____ $9 \times 200 =$ ____	5 $6 \times 5 =$ ____ $6 \times 50 =$ ____ $6 \times 500 =$ ____	6 $7 \times 6 =$ ____ $70 \times 6 =$ ____ $700 \times 6 =$ ____
7 $8 \times 7 =$ ____ $8 \times 70 =$ ____ $8 \times 700 =$ ____	8 $8 \times 8 =$ ____ $8 \times 80 =$ ____ $8 \times 800 =$ ____	9 $9 \times 9 =$ ____ $9 \times 90 =$ ____ $9 \times 900 =$ ____

Use a basic fact to help you find the product.

10 $8 \times 60 =$ ____	11 $4 \times 50 =$ ____	12 $7 \times 90 =$ ____
13 $6 \times 600 =$ ____	14 $9 \times 300 =$ ____	15 $4 \times 500 =$ ____

Problem Solving

Solve the problem. Explain your answer.

16 Seneca's class made two lines to go to lunch. There are the same number of students in each line. Seneca is fifth in his line, and there are 8 students behind him. How many students are in his class? ☐ students

____

____

____

____

____

Name ______________________ Date __________

Spiral Review
Lesson 1

Measurement

Find the distance traveled.

1. 3 hours at 7 miles per hour

   ______ miles

2. 2 hours at 6 miles per hour

   ______ miles

3. 4 hours at 9 miles per hour

   ______ miles

4. 30 minutes at 16 miles per hour

   ______ miles

5. 8 hours at 7 miles per hour

   ______ miles

6. 3 hours at 9 miles per hour

   ______ miles

Number and Operations

Write the expanded form.

7. 561 = 500 + ______ + 1

8. 1,254 = 1,000 + ______ + 50 + 4

9. 3,081 = ______ + 80 + 1

10. 5,692 = 5,000 + ______ + ______ + 2

Find the missing number.

11. 96 − ______ = 68

12. 84 + 26 = ______

13. 203 − 150 = ______

14. ______ + 436 = 872

15. 827 − 32 = ______

16. 27 + ______ = 101

17. 149 + 594 = ______

18. 627 + ______ = 245

Name ______________________ Date ______________

Geometry

Draw the lines of symmetry. Write *None* if the figure has no lines of symmetry.

1. 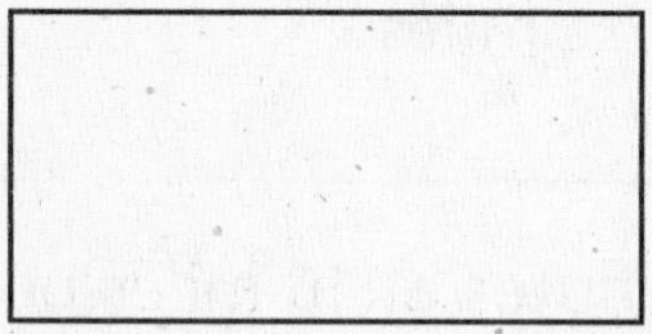

2. 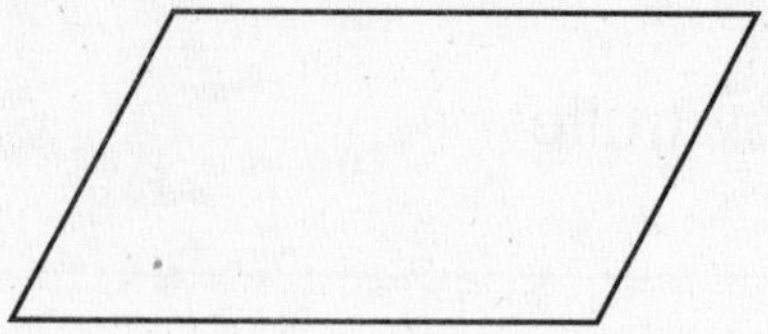

3. 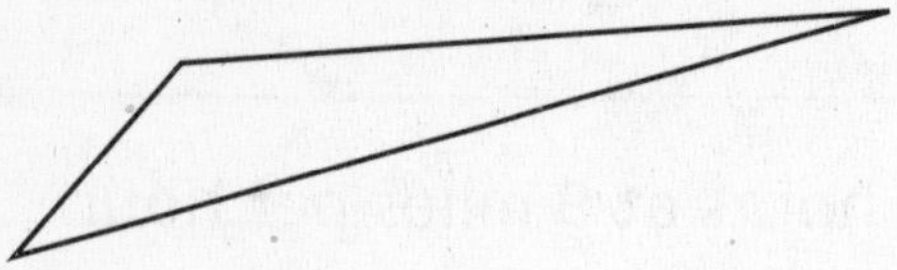

4. 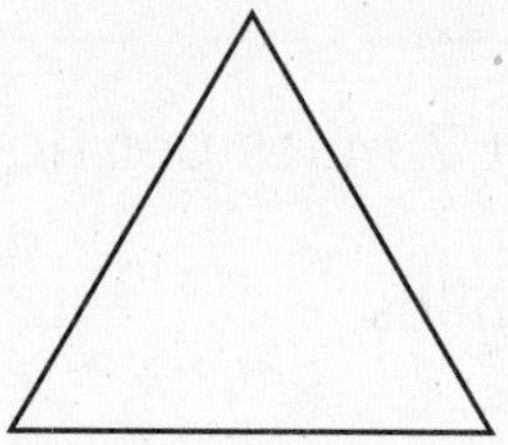

5. 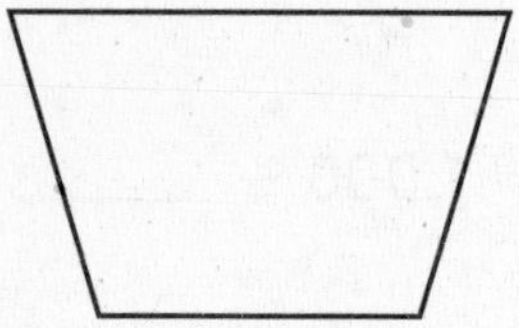

6. 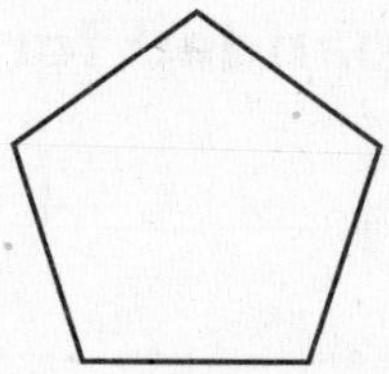

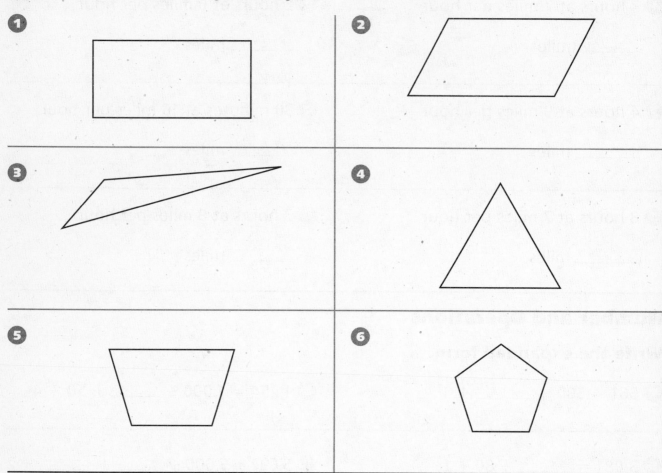

Number and Operations

Write the missing number in each sentence.

7. $6 \times 9 =$ ____

8. $8 \times 7 =$ ____

9. $6 \times 8 =$ ____

10. $9 \times 7 =$ ____

Write the numbers in order from smallest to largest.

11. 896, 891, 902, 911 ______________________

12. 1,043; 1,403; 1,304; 1,430 ______________________

Name ______________________ Date ____________

Algebra

Draw the next 3 figures in each pattern.

1 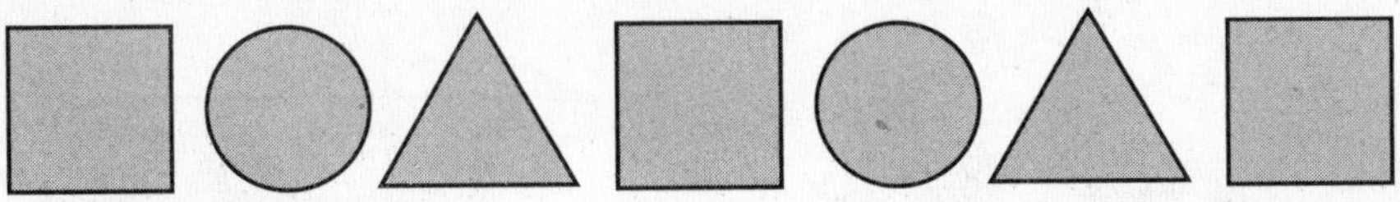 ______ ______ ______

2 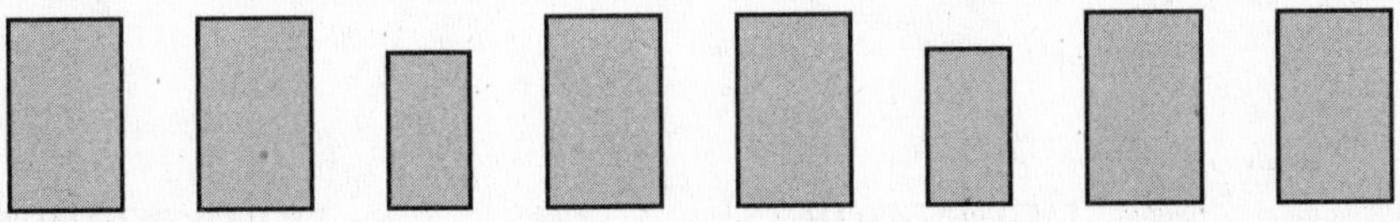 ______ ______ ______

3 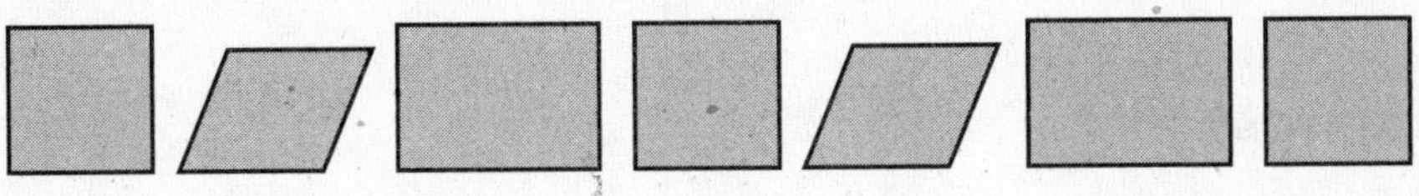 ______ ______ ______

4 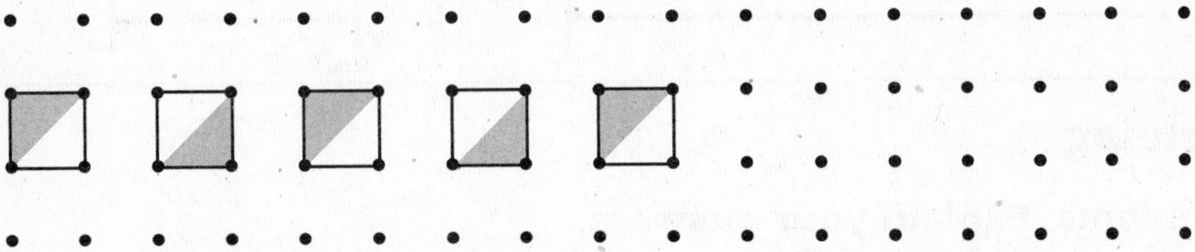

Number and Operations

Write a fraction for the shaded part of each figure.

5 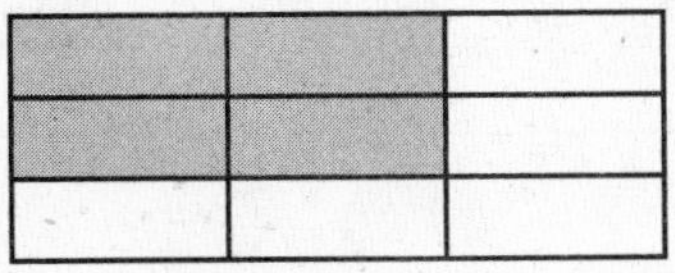 ______

6 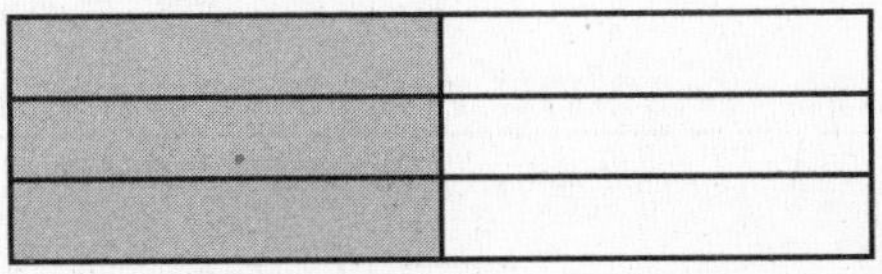 ______

7  ______

8 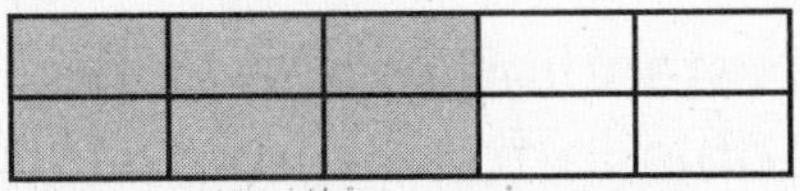 ______

9 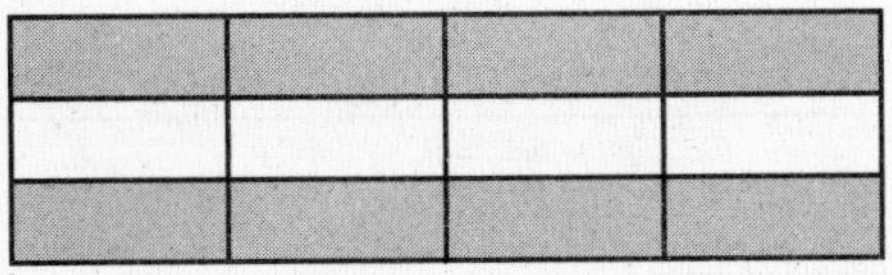 ______

10 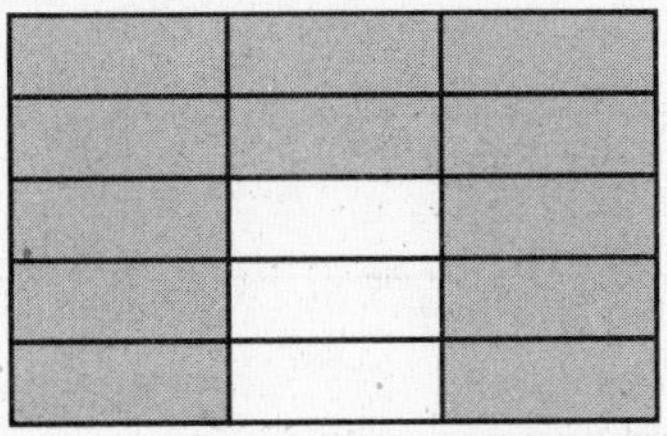 ______

Name ______________________ Date ______________

Spiral Review
Lesson 4

Geometry

Write the number of angles that appear to be right angles for each figure.

1. 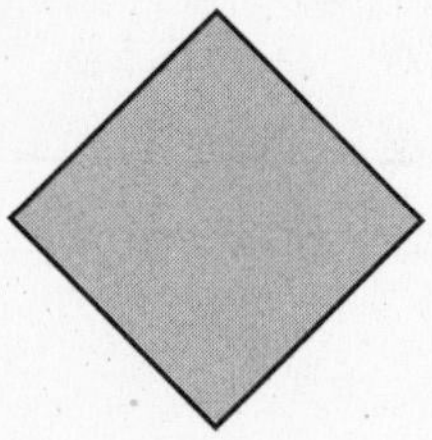

_____ right angle(s)

2. 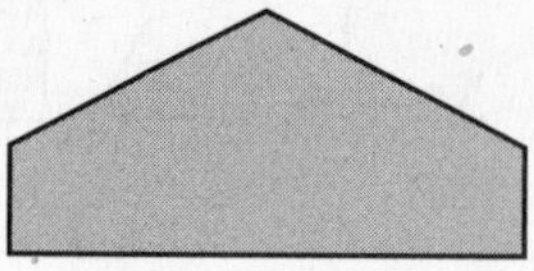

_____ right angle(s)

3. 

_____ right angle(s)

Measurement

Find the length to the nearest inch.

4. length = _____ in.

5. length = _____ in.

Problem Solving

Solve the problems. Explain your answers.

6. Three students are sitting in a row for a photograph. How many different ways can they be arranged?

____

____

____

7. Robert is standing in line to buy a snack. There are 7 people in front of him and 8 people behind him. How many people are waiting in line?

____

____

____

Name ______________________ Date ____________

Spiral Review
Lesson 5

Algebra

Write the rule for going from A to B.

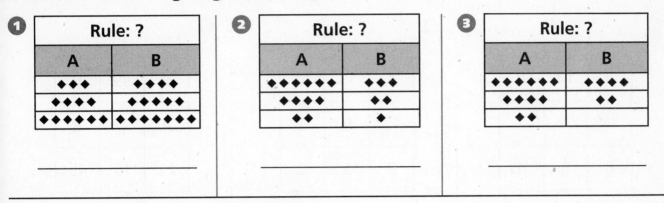

1.

Rule: ?	
A	**B**
◆◆◆	◆◆◆◆
◆◆◆◆	◆◆◆◆◆
◆◆◆◆◆◆	◆◆◆◆◆◆◆

____

2.

Rule: ?	
A	**B**
◆◆◆◆◆◆	◆◆◆
◆◆◆◆	◆◆
◆◆	◆

____

3.

Rule: ?	
A	**B**
◆◆◆◆◆◆	◆◆◆◆
◆◆◆◆	◆◆
◆◆	

____

Data Analysis and Probability

Use the graph for Problems 4–6.

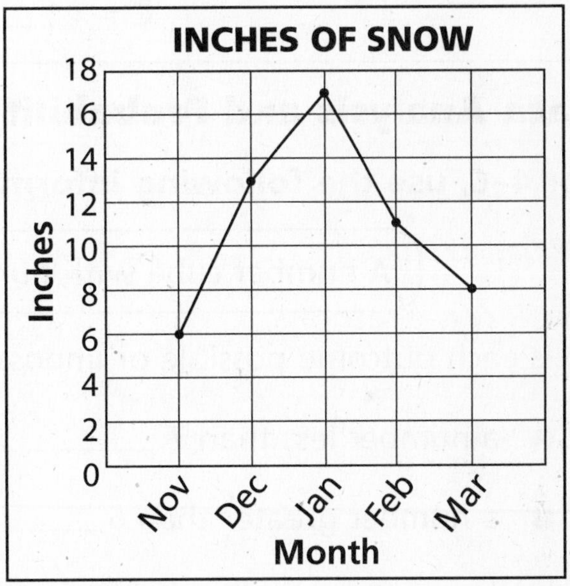

4. How many more inches of snow were there in January than in November?

_______ inches

5. Between which two consecutive months was there the greatest change?

____

6. How many inches of snow fell during the five months?

_______ inches

Reasoning and Proof

7. Write the rule used to create the second magic square from the first.

2	7	6
9	5	1
4	3	8

5	15	13
19	11	3
9	7	17

____

____

____

Name ______________________ Date __________

Algebra

Find the number to complete each magic square.

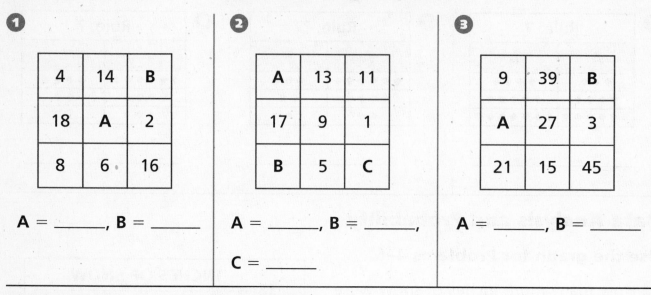

1

4	14	B
18	A	2
8	6	16

A = ______, B = ______

2

A	13	11
17	9	1
B	5	C

A = ______, B = ______,

C = ______

3

9	39	B
A	27	3
21	15	45

A = ______, B = ______

Data Analysis and Probability

For 4–6, use the following information:

A number cube with numbers 1 to 6 is rolled one time.

4 Is each outcome possible or impossible?

A a number less than 7 ______________________

B a number greater than 6 ______________________

C a two-digit number ______________________

D an odd number ______________________

5 Choose the outcome that is more likely.

A an even number or a number greater than 4 ______________________

B an odd number or a number less than 5 ______________________

6 List all possible outcomes for the roll of the number cube.

____

Name ______________________ Date ____________

Algebra

Shade the next 2 figures to continue the pattern. Explain your answer.

1. 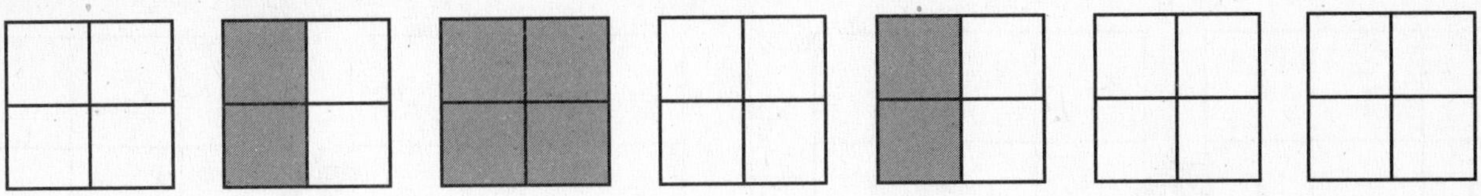

____

____

2. 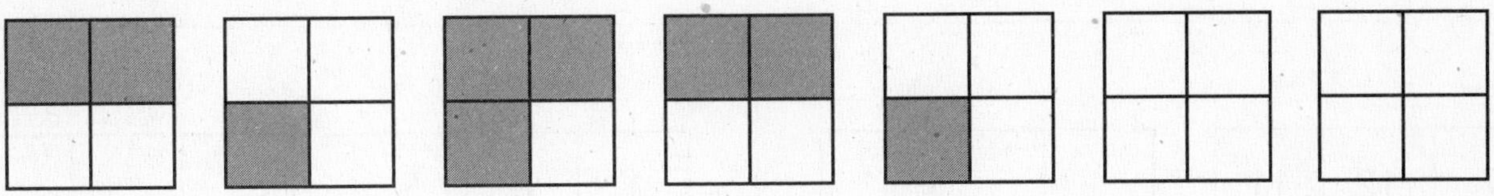

____

____

Problem Solving

Solve the problems. Explain your answers.

3. Jill had $4 left after she bought 3 birthday cards. The birthday cards cost $2 each. How much money did she have before she bought the cards?

____

____

____

4. Miranda left her apartment to exercise by walking up and down the stairwell. She walked down 7 floors. Then, she walked up 3 floors to the 8th floor. Last, she walked up 4 floors to get back to her apartment. Which floor does Miranda live on?

____

____

Name ______________________ Date ____________

Spiral Review
Lesson 8

Number and Operations

Multiply the magic square by the given number.

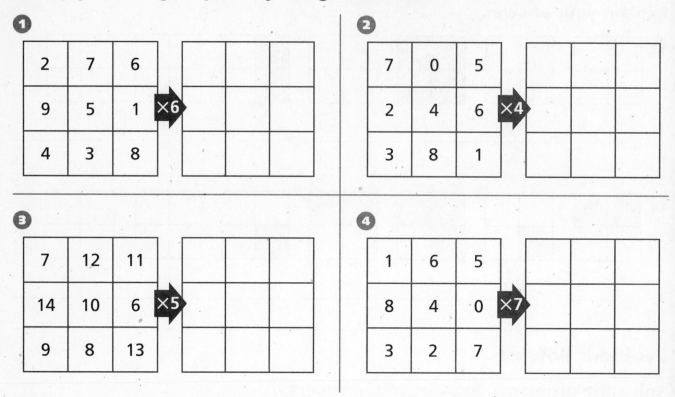

1

2	7	6
9	5	1
4	3	8

×6

2

7	0	5
2	4	6
3	8	1

×4

3

7	12	11
14	10	6
9	8	13

×5

4

1	6	5
8	4	0
3	2	7

×7

Measurement

Find the perimeter and area of each figure.

5 Perimeter = ______ units

Area = ______ square units

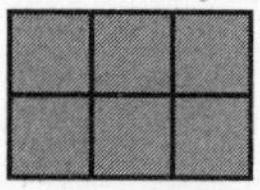

6 Perimeter = ______ units

Area = ______ square units

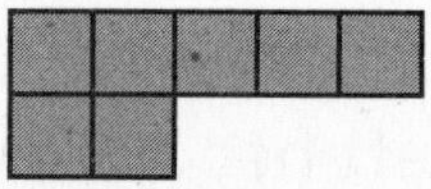

7 Choose the figure that has the smallest perimeter.

A. 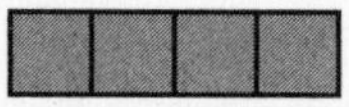

B. 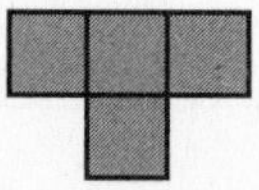

C. 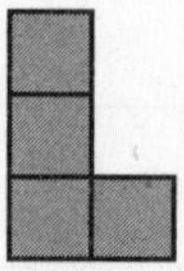

D. 

Name ______________________ Date ____________

Spiral Review
Lesson 1

Measurement

Write *ounces* or *pounds* to complete the sentence so that it makes sense.

1. A stapler weighs about 12 ____________.
2. A ruler weighs about 4 ____________.
3. A volume of an encyclopedia weighs about 5 ____________.
4. A pair of shoes weighs about 32 ____________.
5. A calculator weighs about 6 ____________.
6. A wastebasket weighs about 20 ____________.
7. A student's desk weighs about 18 ____________.
8. A box of chalk weighs about 4 ____________.
9. A carton of books weighs about 30 ____________.
10. A stuffed animal weighs about 2 ____________.

Problem Solving

Use a strategy and solve.

11. Ronnie's bookshelf is 8 feet wide. Each box that he wants to put on the shelf is 1 foot wide. If he puts a box at one end and leaves 6 inches of space between boxes, how many boxes can he fit on the shelf? ____________
12. An apartment house has 12 floors. Herbert lives on Floor 8. He takes the elevator up 3 floors to visit his aunt. Then he walks down 7 floors to visit his grandmother. From there he walks up 3 floors to visit a friend. On what floor does his friend live? ____________
13. A square birthday cake is cut into 16 pieces so that it is a 4-by-4 array of squares. Some friends at the party eat one half of the cake. Later, some other friends eat one half of the pieces that are left. How many pieces of birthday cake have **not** been eaten? ____________

Name ______________________ Date ______________

Spiral Review
Lesson 2

Number and Operations

Write a multiplication sentence for the array.

1. 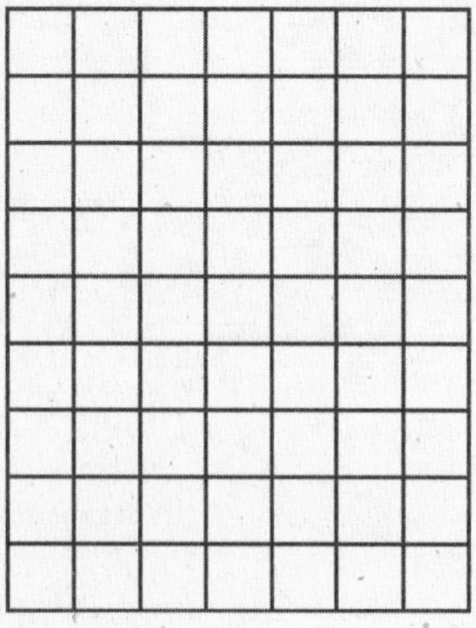

____

2. 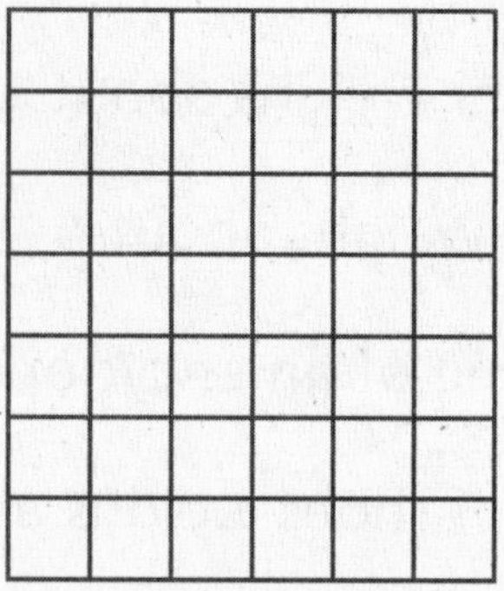

____

Geometry

Find the perimeter and area of the figure. Then draw another figure on the grid that has the same perimeter but a different area.

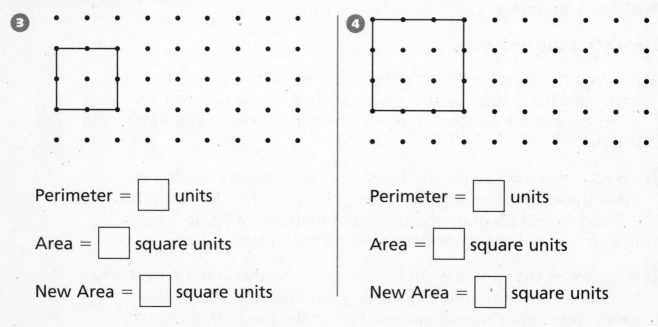

3. 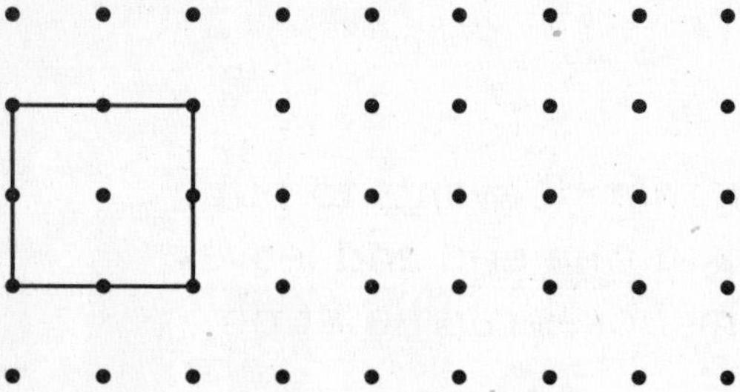

Perimeter = ☐ units

Area = ☐ square units

New Area = ☐ square units

4. 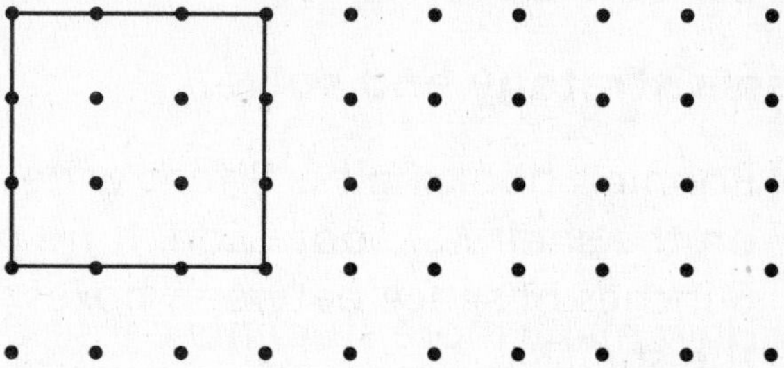

Perimeter = ☐ units

Area = ☐ square units

New Area = ☐ square units

Name ______________________ Date ____________

Spiral Review
Lesson 3

Number and Operations

Add the magic squares. Write the sum for the new square.

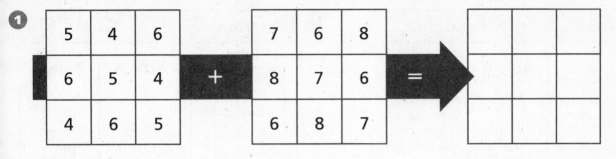

1

5	4	6
6	5	4
4	6	5

\+

7	6	8
8	7	6
6	8	7

=

sum = ______

2

15	10	17
16	14	12
11	18	13

\+

11	6	13
12	10	8
7	14	9

=

sum = ______

Data Analysis and Probability

For 3–5, use the graph.

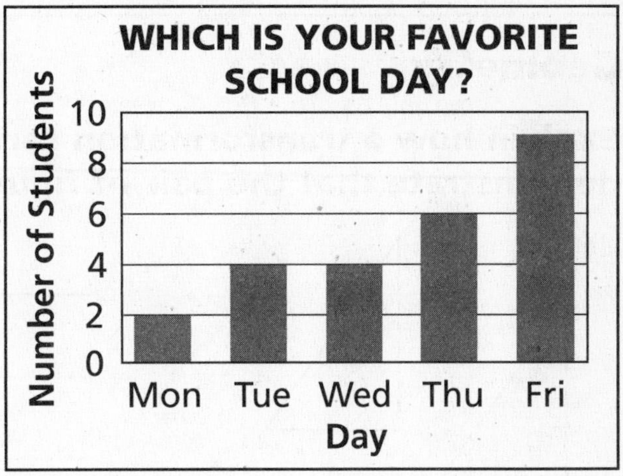

3 How many students answered the question? ________

4 How many more students chose the most popular day than the least popular day? ________

5 Describe a trend you see in the graph.

____

____

Name ______________________ Date ____________

Spiral Review
Lesson 4

Algebra

Complete the card by writing Rule A and Rule B.

1

Front	Back	
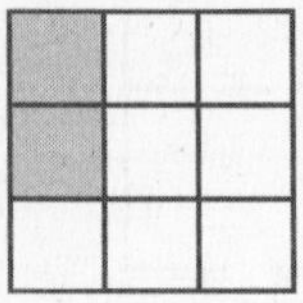	Rule A	Rule B

2

Front	Back	
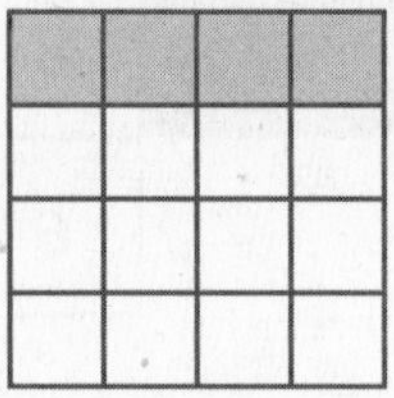	Rule A	Rule B

3

Front	Back	
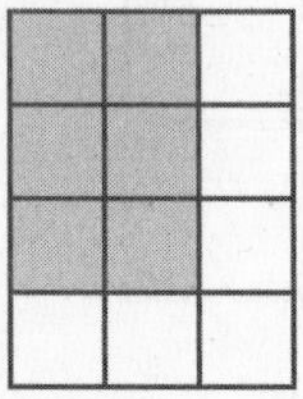	Rule A	Rule B

4

Front	Back	
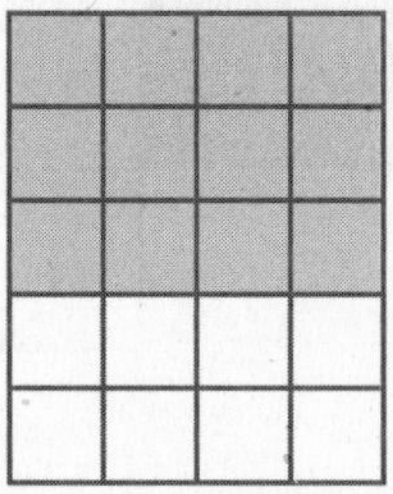	Rule A	Rule B

Geometry

Explain how a transformation can be used to demonstrate that the pair of figures is congruent.

5

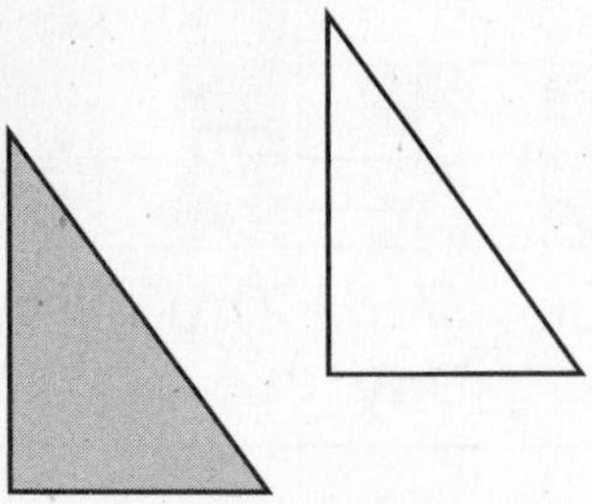

____

____

____

6

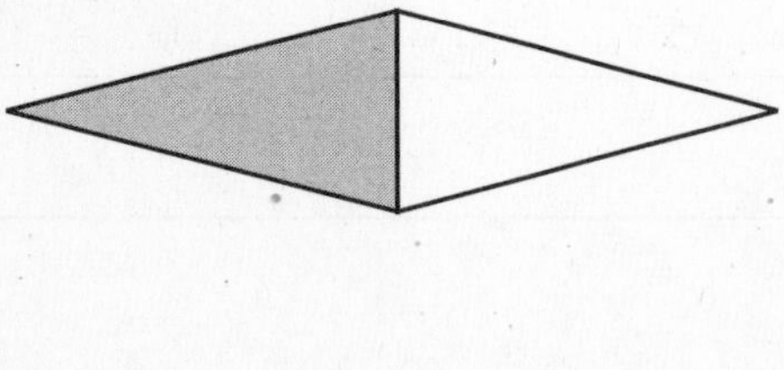

____

____

____

Name ______________________ Date ____________

Spiral Review
Lesson 5

Number and Operations

Find the total number of items in the set.

1. 3 cartons of books; each carton has 7 books. ________
2. 8 bags of pears; each bag has 7 pears. ________
3. 2 boxes of buttons; each box has 7×7 buttons. ________
4. 2 crates of oranges; each crate has $7 \times 7 \times 7$ oranges. ________
5. 13 boxes of sweaters; each box has 7 sweaters. ________
6. 12 cases of juice; each case has 7×7 bottles. ________
7. 9 cases of tissue boxes; each case has $7 \times 7 \times 7$ boxes. ________
8. 15 cartons of cereal; each carton has 7×7 cereal boxes. ________
9. 18 crates of apples; each crate has $7 \times 7 \times 7$ apples. ________
10. 52 boxes of peanuts; each box has 7×7 bags of peanuts. ________

Measurement

Measure the line segment. Write the length to the nearest centimeter.

11. ____________________ ☐ cm
12. __________________________________ ☐ cm
13. __________________________ ☐ cm
14. ________________ ☐ cm
15. _____________________________________ ☐ cm
16. __________ ☐ cm
17. _____________ ☐ cm

Name ______________________ Date ____________

Spiral Review
Lesson 6

Algebra

Find a rule for the set of cards.

1.

FRONT	BACK
7	21

FRONT	BACK
8	24

FRONT	BACK
9	27

____

2.

FRONT	BACK
28	7

FRONT	BACK
36	9

FRONT	BACK
16	4

____

3.

FRONT	BACK
18	11

FRONT	BACK
23	16

FRONT	BACK
31	24

____

Problem Solving

Use a strategy and solve.

4. A small pool holds 500 gallons of water. It takes 1 minute to put 5 gallons of water into the pool. How long, in hours and minutes, will it take to fill the pool? ____________

5. Four boys and 4 girls volunteer for a committee that will have 1 boy and 1 girl. How many different committees are possible? ____________

Name ______________________ Date ____________

Spiral Review
Lesson 7

Number and Operations

Write a fraction for the shaded part of the figure.

1. 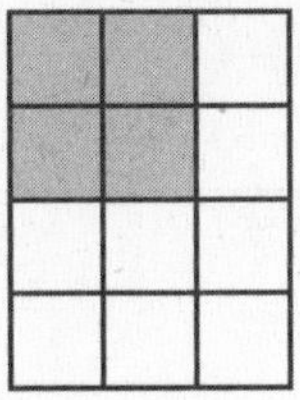

2. 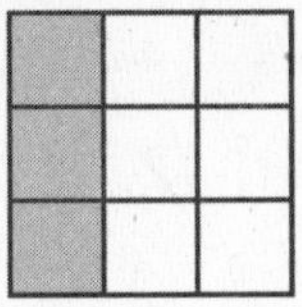

3. 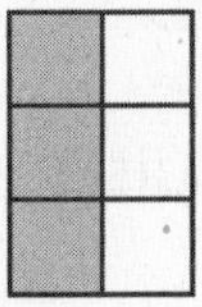

4. 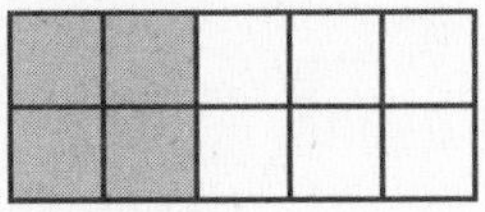

5. 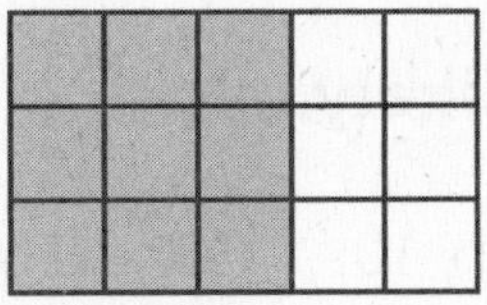

6. 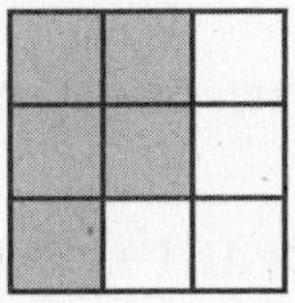

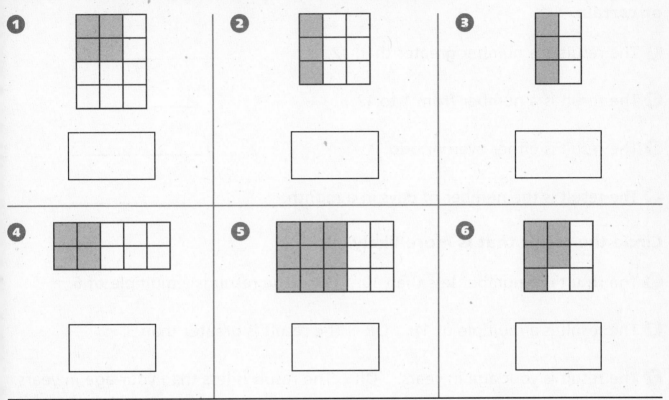

Reasoning and Proof

Solve.

7. Ron is packing 185 books at the bookstore. One carton holds 20 books. How many full cartons can he pack? How many books will be left over?

____

8. There are 4 bus seats in each row. Passengers fill up each row before starting a new row. If there are 39 passengers on the bus, how many rows are filled? How many passengers are in the last row?

____

Name ______________________ Date ____________

Spiral Review
Lesson 8

Data Analysis and Probability

You spin a spinner numbered 1–12. Write *impossible* or *certain*.

1. The result is a number greater than 12. ____________

2. The result is a number from 1 to 12. ____________

3. The result is either even or odd. ____________

4. The result is the number of days in a month. ____________

Circle the result that is more likely.

5. The result is a number less than 10. OR The result is a multiple of 6.

6. The result is a multiple of 11. OR The result is greater than 3.

7. The result is your age in years. OR The result is less than your age in years.

Geometry

Write *triangle, quadrilateral, pentagon* or *none of them.*

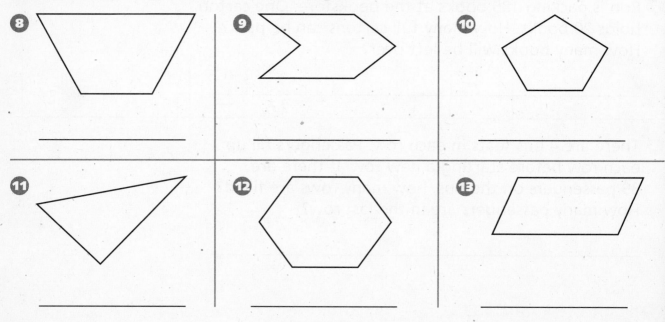

8. 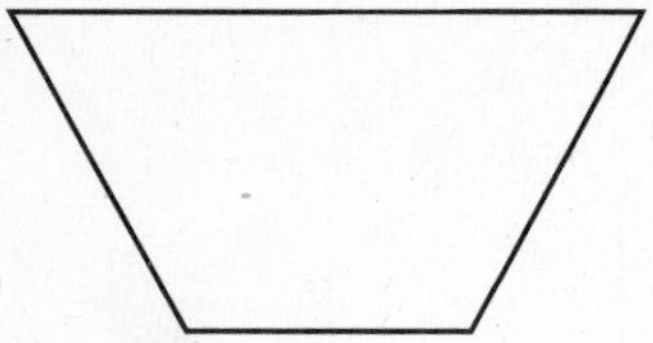

____

9. 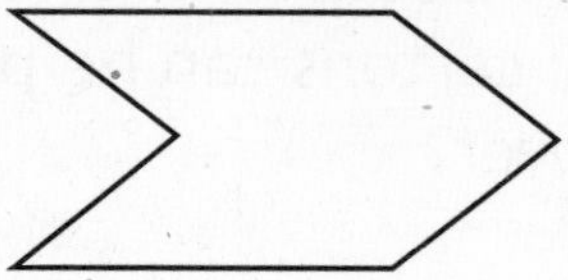

____

10. 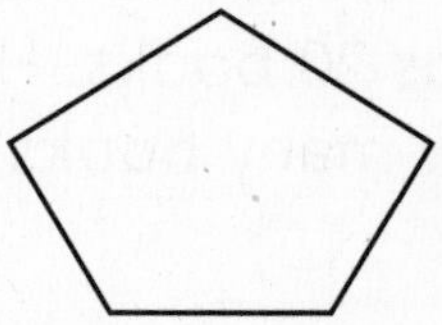

____

11. 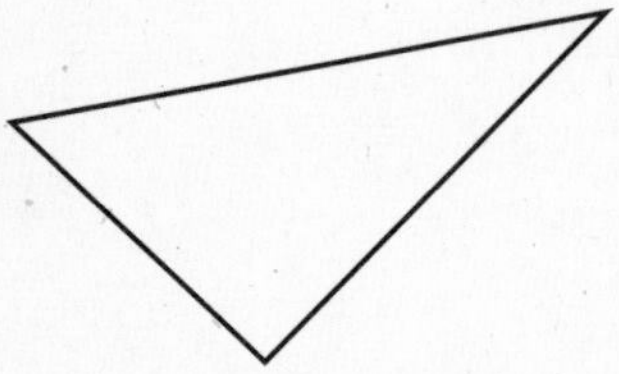

____

12. 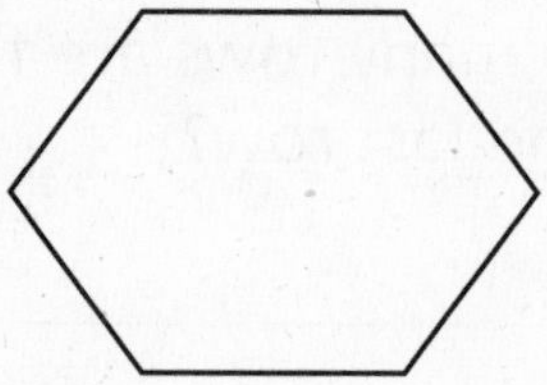

____

13. 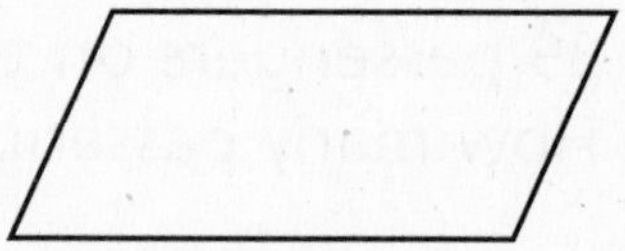

____

Name ______________________ Date ______________

Spiral Review
Lesson 9

Algebra

Write a multiplication sentence to find the number of tiles in the picture.

1. 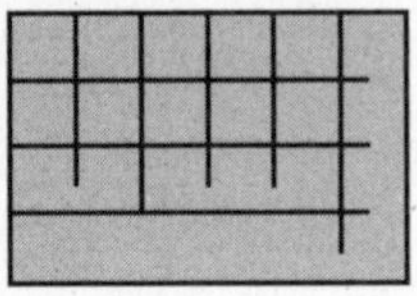

[ ]

2. 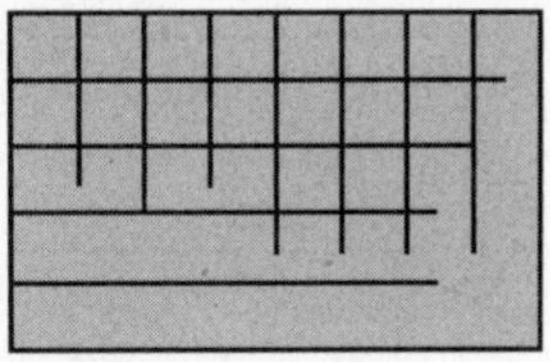

[ ]

3. 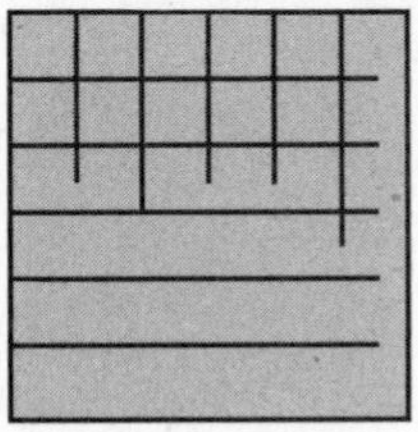

[ ]

4. 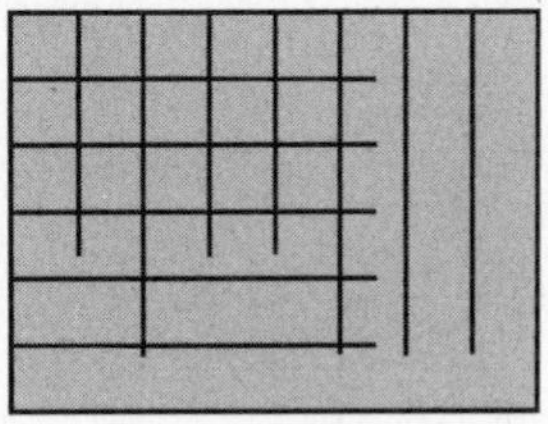

[ ]

Measurement

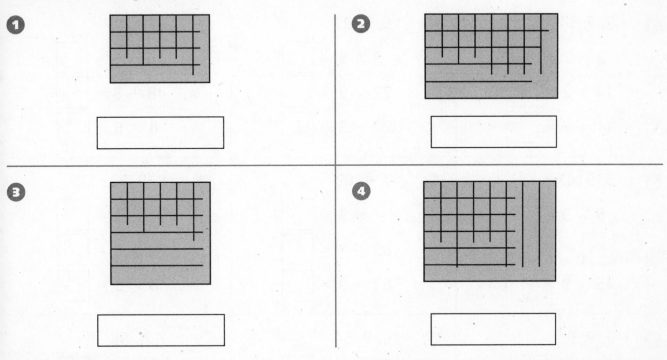

Write the temperature shown on the thermometer.

5. 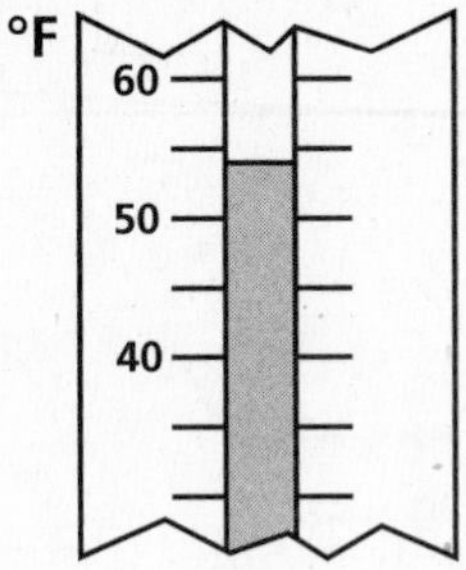

[ ] °F

6. 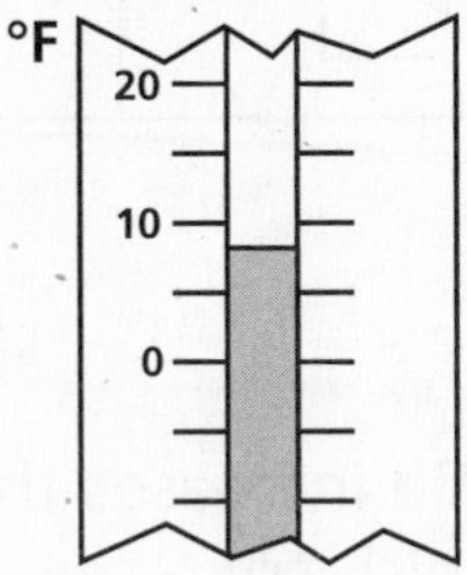

[ ] °F

7. 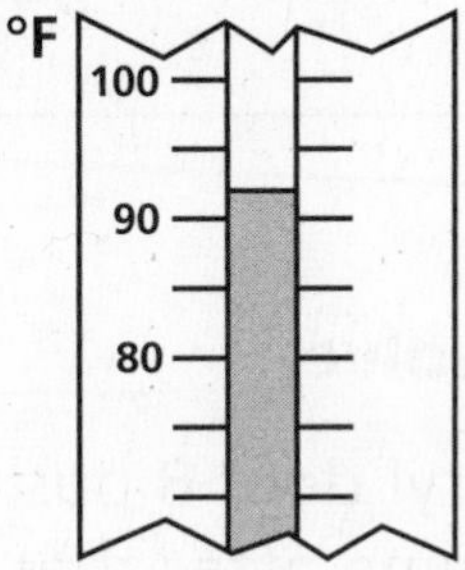

[ ] °F

8. 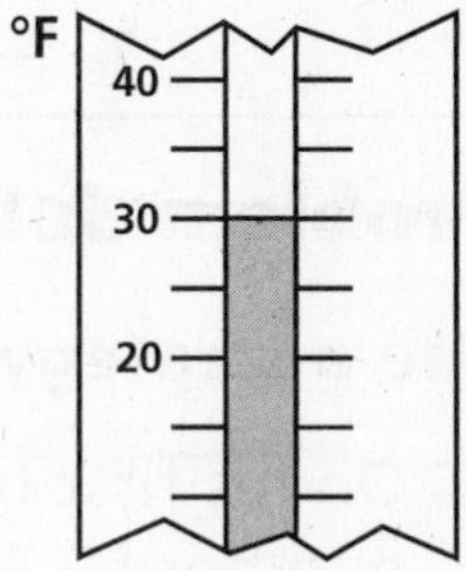

[ ] °F

Write the difference between the high and low temperatures.

9. high temperature 62°F, low temperature 38°F [ ] °F

10. high temperature 100°F, low temperature 16°F [ ] °F

Name ______________________ Date ____________

Number and Operations

Use the fact family to complete the number sentences.

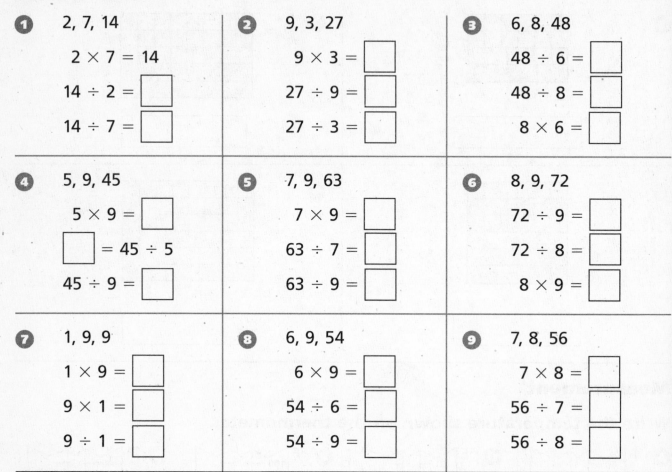

1 2, 7, 14 2 × 7 = 14 14 ÷ 2 = ☐ 14 ÷ 7 = ☐	**2** 9, 3, 27 9 × 3 = ☐ 27 ÷ 9 = ☐ 27 ÷ 3 = ☐	**3** 6, 8, 48 48 ÷ 6 = ☐ 48 ÷ 8 = ☐ 8 × 6 = ☐
4 5, 9, 45 5 × 9 = ☐ ☐ = 45 ÷ 5 45 ÷ 9 = ☐	**5** 7, 9, 63 7 × 9 = ☐ 63 ÷ 7 = ☐ 63 ÷ 9 = ☐	**6** 8, 9, 72 72 ÷ 9 = ☐ 72 ÷ 8 = ☐ 8 × 9 = ☐
7 1, 9, 9 1 × 9 = ☐ 9 × 1 = ☐ 9 ÷ 1 = ☐	**8** 6, 9, 54 6 × 9 = ☐ 54 ÷ 6 = ☐ 54 ÷ 9 = ☐	**9** 7, 8, 56 7 × 8 = ☐ 56 ÷ 7 = ☐ 56 ÷ 8 = ☐

Problem Solving

Use a strategy and solve.

10. On his first try, Darryl does 8 push-ups. He increases the number by 2 each time after that. On which try will Darryl do 20 push-ups? ☐

11. Robin throws a ball 120 feet. Each throw after that is half the distance of the one before. When she has thrown the ball 4 times, how many feet will she have thrown it in all? ☐

Name ______________________ Date ______________

Spiral Review
Lesson 1

Number and Operations

Divide the magic square by the number shown.

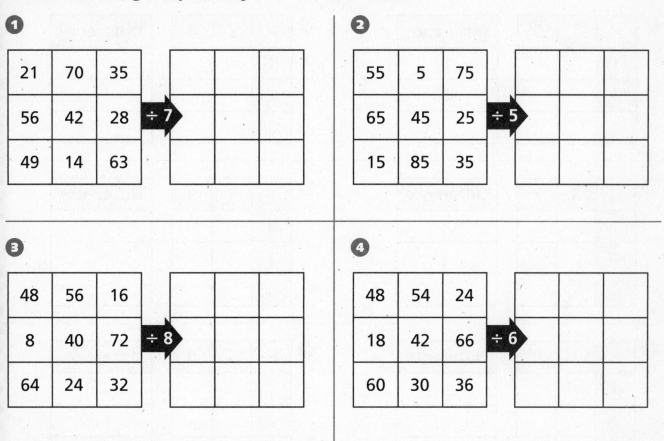

1 ÷ 7

21	70	35
56	42	28
49	14	63

2 ÷ 5

55	5	75
65	45	25
15	85	35

3 ÷ 8

48	56	16
8	40	72
64	24	32

4 ÷ 6

48	54	24
18	42	66
60	30	36

Problem Solving

Solve the problem. Explain your answer.

5 How many squares of any size can you find in this grid?

____

6 A restaurant has square tables that seat one person on each side. For parties, they put them together to make long tables. What is the greatest number of people that can sit at a long table made from 9 square tables?

____

____

Name ______________________ Date ____________

Algebra

Complete each multiplication table.

1.

×	4	5
1		
2		
3		

Difference
1
2

2.

×	3	4
1		
2		
3		

Difference

3.

×	5	7
1		
2		
3		

Difference

4.

×	7	9
1		
2		
3		

Difference

5.

×	2	6
1		
2		
3		

Difference

6.

×	5	9
1		
2		
3		

Difference

Measurement

Find the difference between the temperatures.

7. 72°F and 39°F ______

8. 81°F and 29°F ______

9. 18°F and 7°F ______

10. 51°F and 32°F ______

11. 40°F and 27°F ______

12. 104°F and 75°F ______

Name ____________________ Date ____________

Spiral Review
Lesson 3

Number and Operations

Complete the multiplications for the array.

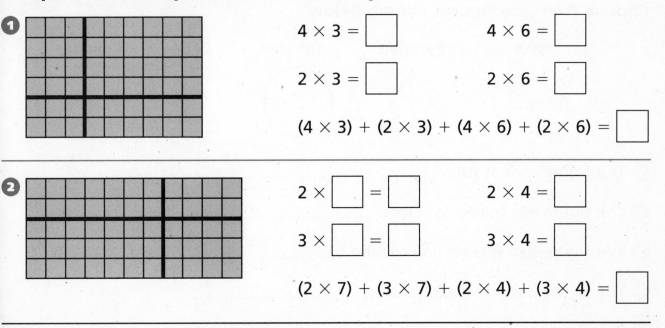

1

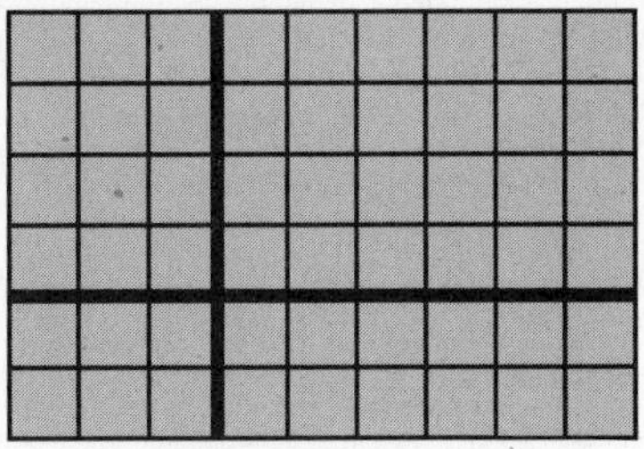

$4 \times 3 = \square$ $4 \times 6 = \square$

$2 \times 3 = \square$ $2 \times 6 = \square$

$(4 \times 3) + (2 \times 3) + (4 \times 6) + (2 \times 6) = \square$

2

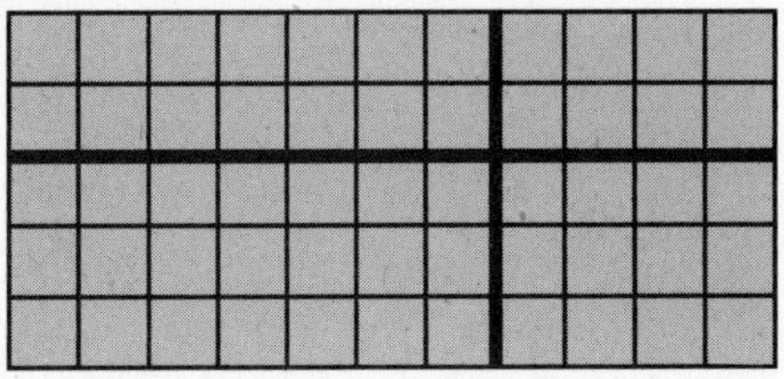

$2 \times \square = \square$ $2 \times 4 = \square$

$3 \times \square = \square$ $3 \times 4 = \square$

$(2 \times 7) + (3 \times 7) + (2 \times 4) + (3 \times 4) = \square$

Data Analysis and Probability

For 3–6, use the pictograph.

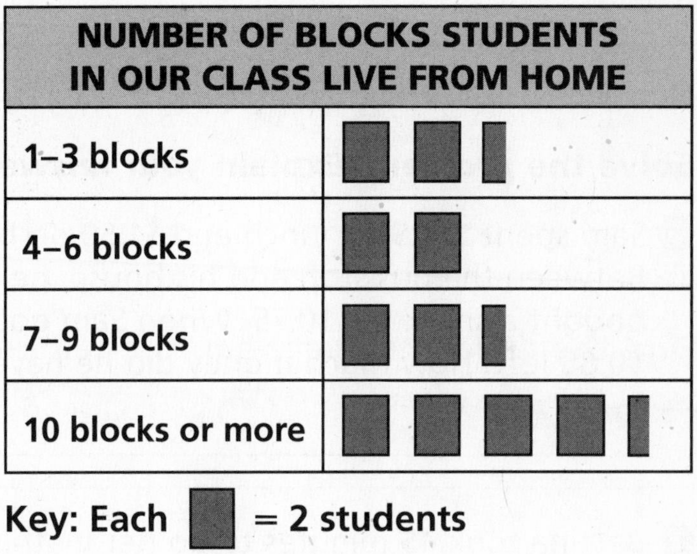

NUMBER OF BLOCKS STUDENTS IN OUR CLASS LIVE FROM HOME
1–3 blocks
4–6 blocks
7–9 blocks
10 blocks or more
Key: Each
= 2 students

3 How many students are in the class?

____

4 How many students live at least 7 blocks from school?

____

5 How many students live fewer than 10 blocks from school?

____

6 Students who live no more than 6 blocks from school usually walk. How many students usually walk to school?

____

Name ______________________ Date ______________

Geometry

Write the names of the figures that fit each description. Choose from the figures shown below.

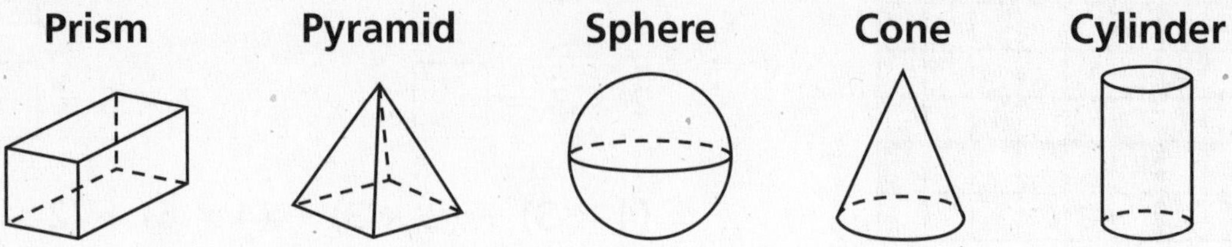

1. The figure cannot roll. ______________________

2. The figure has triangular faces. ______________________

3. The figure has at least one circular base. ______________________

4. The figure has one base. ______________________

5. The figure has two bases that are the same size and shape.

____

Problem Solving

Solve the problem. Explain your answer.

6. Sam spent $1.25 on lunch and $1.50 on bus fare home. Between the bus stop and his house, he stopped and bought a snack for $0.75. When Sam got home, he had $0.85 left. How much money did he have before lunch?

____

____

7. Bettina took 45 minutes to do her math homework and 30 minutes to do her social studies assignment. She finished at 5:30 P.M. At what time did she start?

____

____

Name ______________________ Date ______________

Spiral Review
Lesson 5

Data Analysis and Probability

For 1–5, use the table or the bar graph.

MONEY SPENT IN SCHOOL VENDING MACHINES DURING ONE WEEK	
Mon	$52
Tue	$28
Wed	$35
Thu	$48
Fri	$69

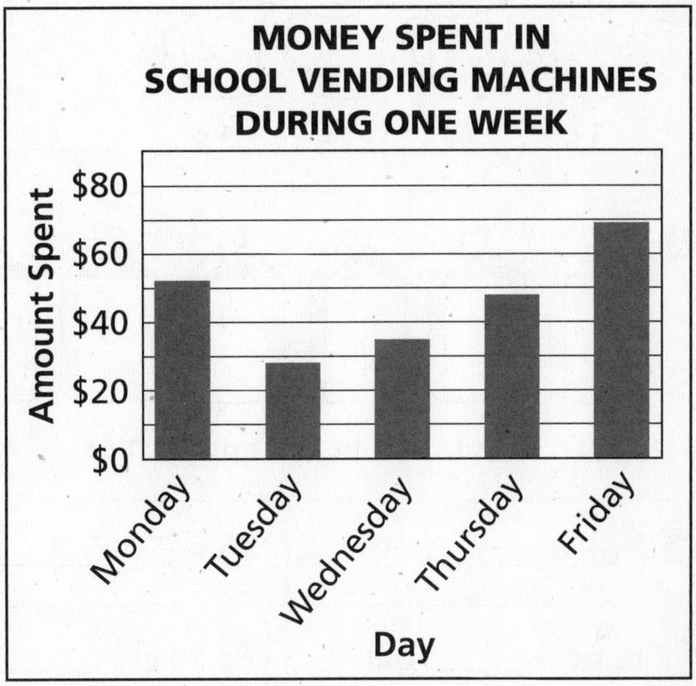

1. What is the difference between the greatest and least amounts spent? ______________

2. Describe how spending changed during the week.

____

____

Reasoning and Proof

There are four houses on one side of a street. John's house is between Rachel's and LaToya's. Rachel's house is next to Craig's.

3. If Rachel lives in the first house on the left, who lives in the first house on the right? ______________

Name ______________________ Date ____________

Measurement

Write the equivalent measure.

1. 

1 c 1 c 1 c 1 c = _____ pt

2. 

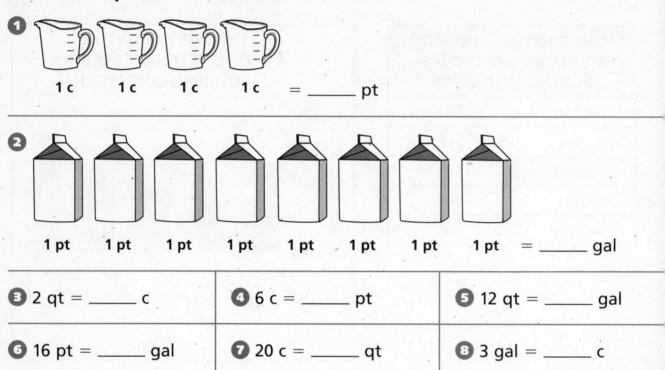

1 pt 1 pt 1 pt 1 pt 1 pt 1 pt 1 pt 1 pt = _____ gal

3. 2 qt = _____ c	4. 6 c = _____ pt	5. 12 qt = _____ gal
6. 16 pt = _____ gal	7. 20 c = _____ qt	8. 3 gal = _____ c

Problem Solving

For 9–10, solve the problem. Explain your answer.

9. There are 3 flavors of ice cream and 4 types of cones. How many different flavor-cone combinations can you make?

10. A burger shop sells 7 hamburgers for every 3 cheeseburgers. If they sell 245 hamburgers this week, how many cheeseburgers do they sell?

Name ____________________ Date ____________

Spiral Review
Lesson 7

Number and Operations

Divide.

1. 80 ÷ 10 ____	2. 120 ÷ 10 ____	3. 550 ÷ 10 ____	4. 600 ÷ 10 ____
5. 130 ÷ 10 ____	6. 10)320 ____	7. 10)90 ____	8. 10)820 ____
9. 10)1,300 ____	10. 2,400 ÷ 10 ____	11. 570 ÷ 10 ____	12. 10)1,110 ____
13. 790 ÷ 10 ____	14. 10)1,000 ____	15. 10)4,200 ____	16. 10)3,120 ____

Data Analysis and Probability

Make a list of all possible outcomes for each experiment.

17. Spin the spinner once.

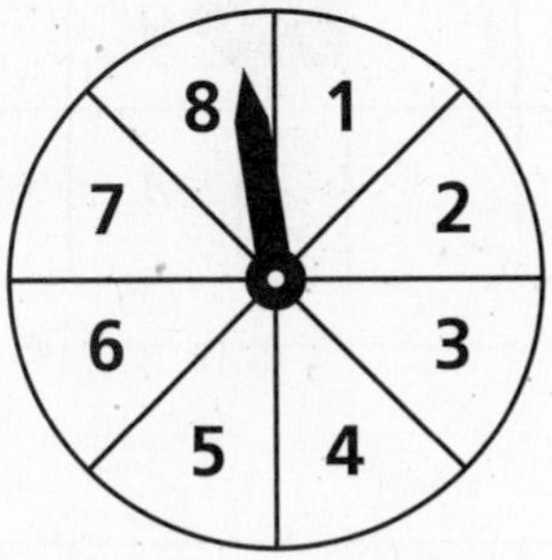

____

18. Toss the paper drinking cup in the air, and record how it lands.

____

19. Toss the number cube one time. The faces are numbered in order, beginning with 3.

____

Name ______________________ Date ____________

Spiral Review
Lesson 8

Algebra

Complete the sentences.

1. $2 \times 9 = 18$

   $18 \div 2 = \square$

2. $4 \times 5 = 20$

   $20 \div 4 = \square$

3. $7 \times 5 = 35$

   $35 \div \square = 5$

4. $6 \times 7 = \square$

   $42 \div 7 = 6$

5. $8 \times 9 = 72$

   $72 \div \square = 9$

6. $6 \times \square = 54$

   $54 \div 6 = 9$

7. $9 \times \square = 81$

   $81 \div \square = 9$

8. $7 \times \square = 63$

   $63 \div 9 = \square$

9. $8 \times \square = 64$

   $64 \div \square = 8$

Reasoning and Proof

Complete each magic square.

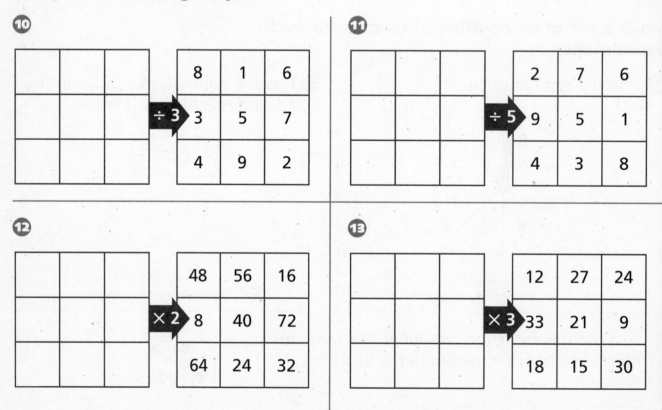

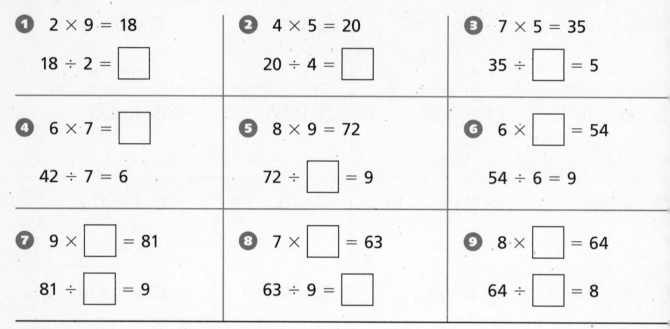

10.

÷ 3 →

8	1	6
3	5	7
4	9	2

11.

÷ 5 →

2	7	6
9	5	1
4	3	8

12.

× 2 →

48	56	16
8	40	72
64	24	32

13.

× 3 →

12	27	24
33	21	9
18	15	30

Name ______________________________ Date ______________

Spiral Review
Lesson 9

Number and Operations

Make as many full columns as possible. Then fill in the missing number of rows, columns, and leftover tiles.

1. Arrange 29 tiles into columns of no more than 3 tiles.

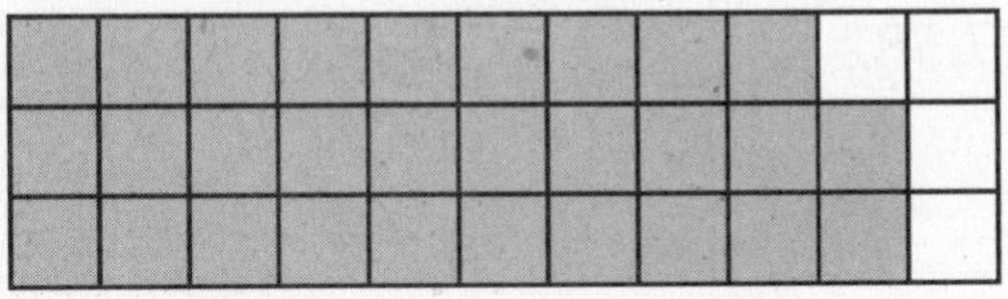

Rows: _____

Columns: _____

Leftover tiles: _____

2. Arrange 18 tiles into columns of no more than 4 tiles.

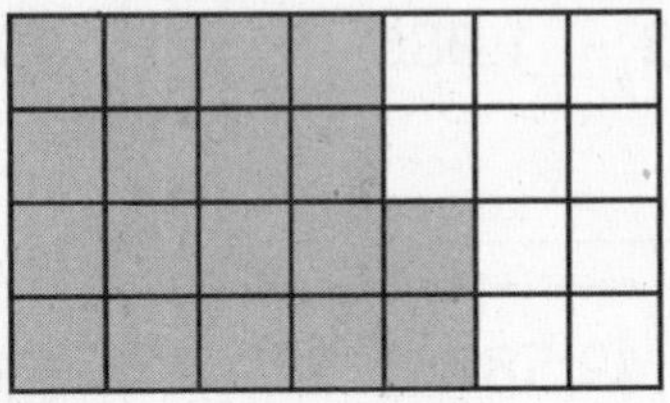

Rows: _____

Columns: _____

Leftover tiles: _____

Geometry

Draw all lines of symmetry for the figure. If the figure has no lines of symmetry, write *none*.

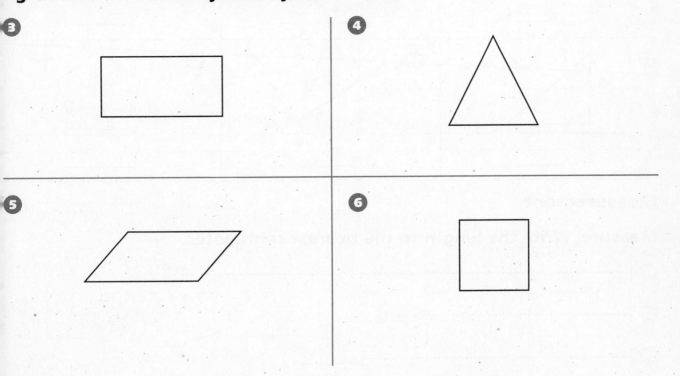

3.

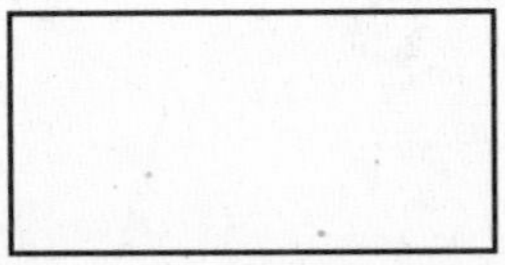

4.

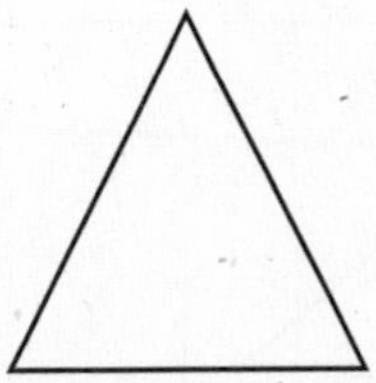

5.

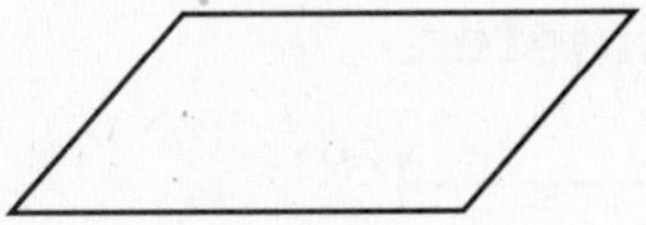

6.

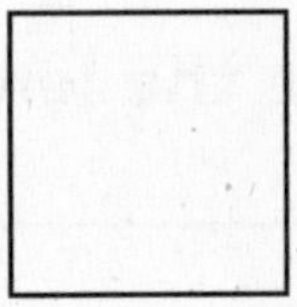

Name ______________________ Date ______________

Spiral Review
Lesson 1

Number and Operations

Find the sum or difference.

1. 39,524 + 1,853 ______

2. 83,845 + 3,850 ______

3. 58,411 − 3,945 ______

4. 7,403 − 1,086 ______

5. 49,103 − 27,582 ______

6. 65,004 + 27,396 ______

7. $\begin{array}{r} 49{,}582 \\ 10{,}547 \\ +\ 6{,}194 \\ \hline \end{array}$

8. $\begin{array}{r} 597 \\ 4{,}493 \\ +32{,}686 \\ \hline \end{array}$

9. $\begin{array}{r} 44{,}972 \\ 1{,}895 \\ +84{,}885 \\ \hline \end{array}$

Geometry

Write *acute, right,* or *obtuse* to describe the appearance of each angle.

10. 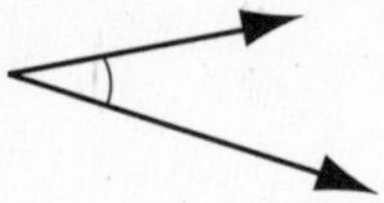

______

11. 

______

12. 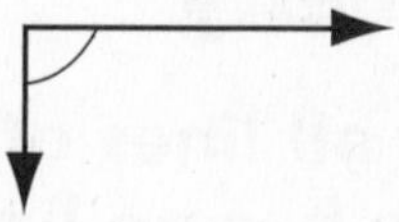

______

13. 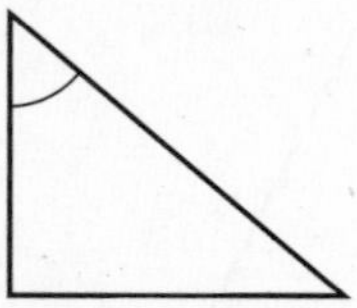

______

14. 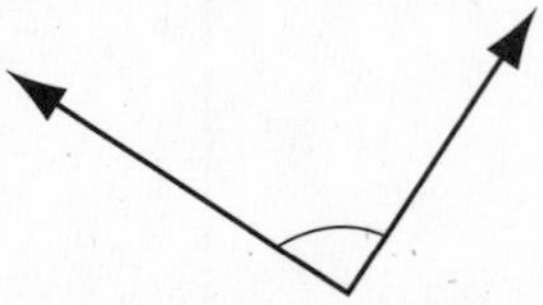

______

15. 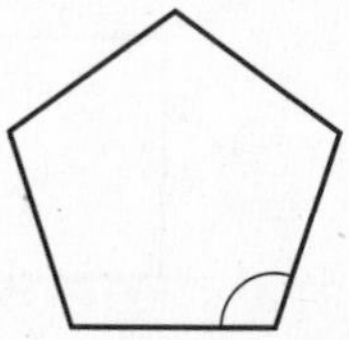

______

Measurement

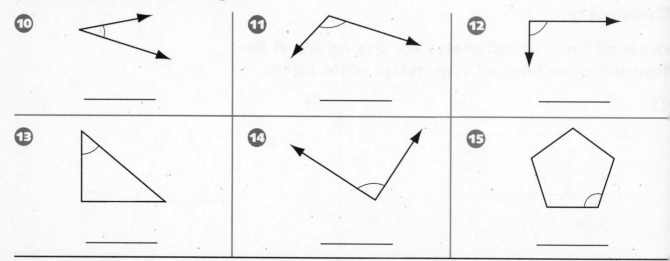

Measure. Write the length to the nearest centimeter.

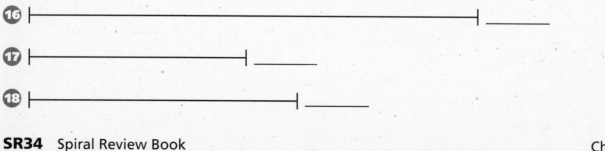

16. |————————————————————| ______

17. |——————————| ______

18. |————————————| ______

Name ____________________ Date ____________

Spiral Review
Lesson 2

Number and Operations

Write the product or quotient.

1. 5×7 ______
2. $42 \div 6$ ______
3. 9×3 ______
4. $32 \div 8$ ______
5. $81 \div 9$ ______
6. $56 \div 8$ ______
7. 6×8 ______
8. 8×9 ______
9. $63 \div 7$ ______
10. 4×10 ______
11. $49 \div 7$ ______
12. $64 \div 8$ ______
13. 3×7 ______
14. $45 \div 9$ ______
15. 9×6 ______
16. $36 \div 6$ ______
17. 5×6 ______
18. $72 \div 8$ ______
19. 10×7 ______
20. $56 \div 7$ ______

Problem Solving

Solve the problem. Explain your answer.

21. If Jenny keeps saving at the same rate, how much will she have at the end of 10 weeks?

Jenny's Savings				
Week	1	2	3	4
Amount	$5.00	$7.50	$10.00	$12.50

____

____

Name ______________________ Date ____________

Geometry

Use the triangles below. You may use the same triangle more than once. Tell which triangle or triangles you can move to form the figure shown, and whether each move is a translation, rotation, reflection, or a combination of these.

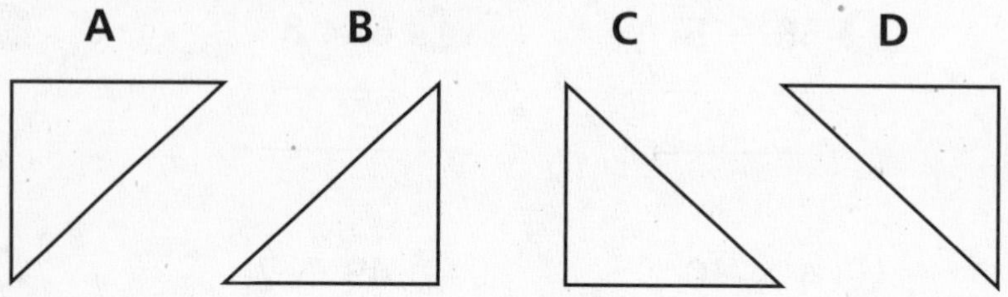

1. 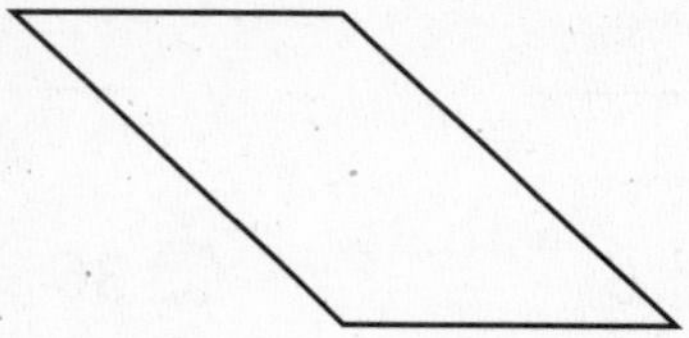

____

2. 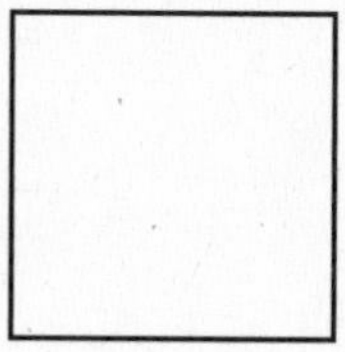

____

3. 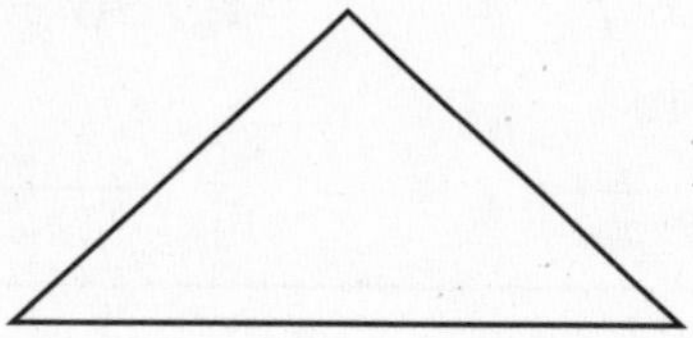

____

4. 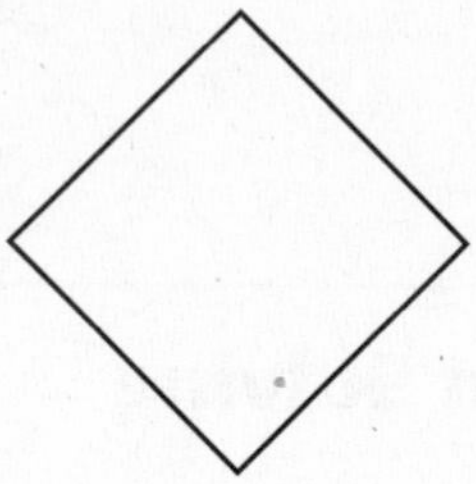

____

Problem Solving

5. Solve the problem. Explain your answer.

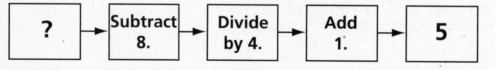

?	→	Subtract 8.	→	Divide by 4.	→	Add 1.	→	5

____

____

Name ______________________ Date ____________

Geometry

Draw all the lines of symmetry for each figure. If there are no lines of symmetry, write *none*.

1. 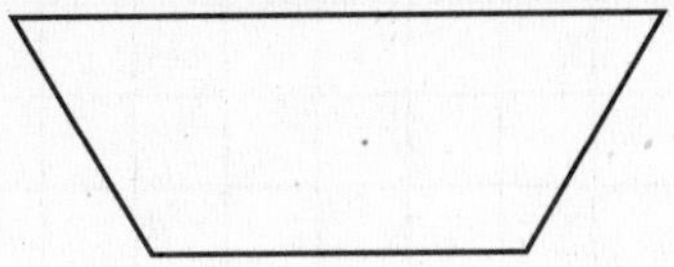

2. 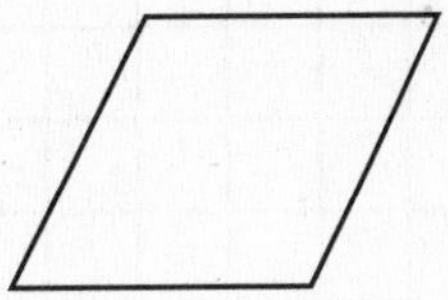

Data Analysis and Probability

3. Complete the bar graph using the data in the table.

FAVORITE OLYMPIC EVENTS	
Event	**Number of Students**
Diving	15
Gymnastics	35
Hockey	20
Skiing	25
Track	60

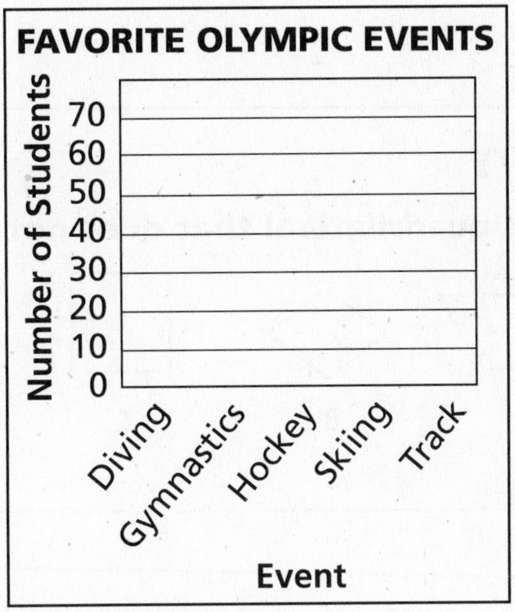

Use the bar graph you made for Problems 4 and 5.

4. If each student voted once, how many students were polled? ________

5. Which event received the second most number of votes? Explain.

____

____

____

Name ______________________________ Date ______________

Number and Operations

Find the number of squares in each array.

1

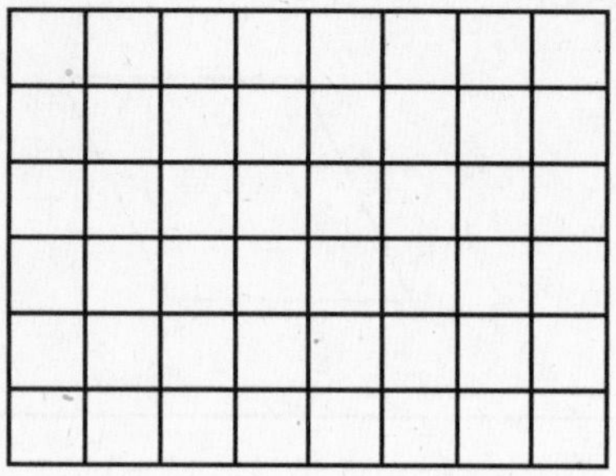

_______ squares

2

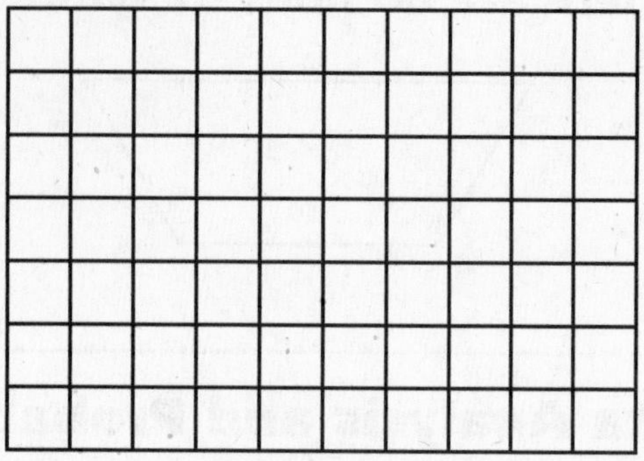

_______ squares

Geometry

Circle the quadrilateral that does not belong. Explain.

3

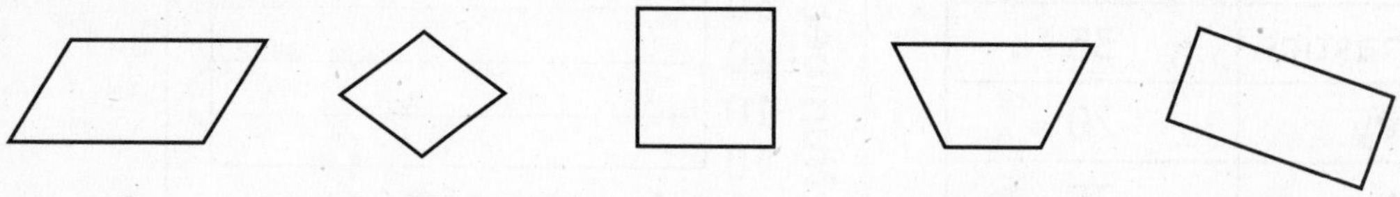

A B C D E

____

Measurement

Write the number of cubes in each figure.

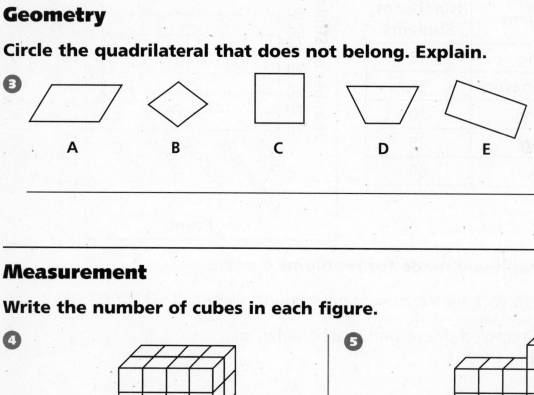

4

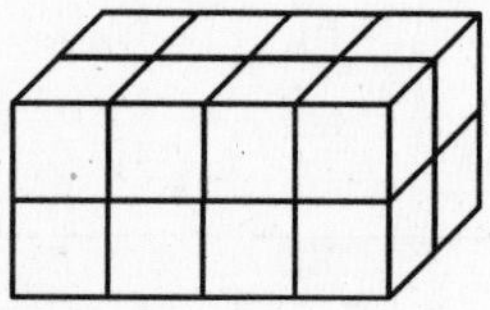

_______ cubes

5

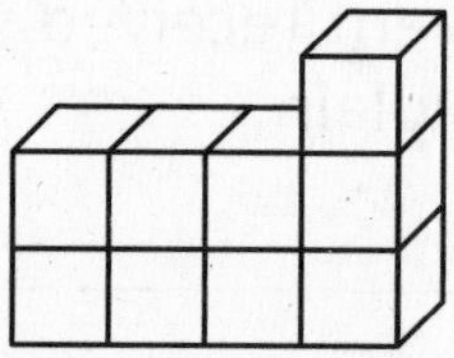

_______ cubes

Name ______________________ Date ______________

Algebra

Find the missing factor.

1. $9 \times$ ____ $= 27$
2. $6 \times$ ____ $= 24$
3. $7 \times$ ____ $= 49$
4. $81 = 9 \times$ ____
5. $3 \times$ ____ $= 30$
6. ____ $\times 8 = 48$
7. $5 \times$ ____ $= 40$
8. ____ $\times 6 = 42$
9. ____ $\times 9 = 36$

Problem Solving

Solve the problem. Explain your answer.

10. A baseball stadium has 34 seating areas. Each area has 185 seats. How many seats are there in the stadium?

____

____

Number and Operations

Find the number of squares in each array.

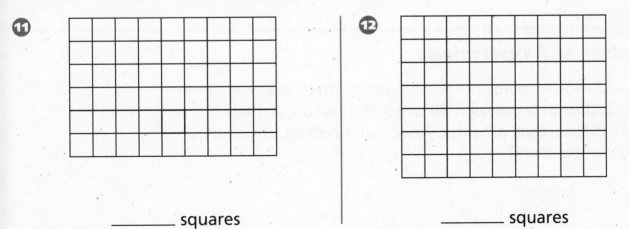

11.
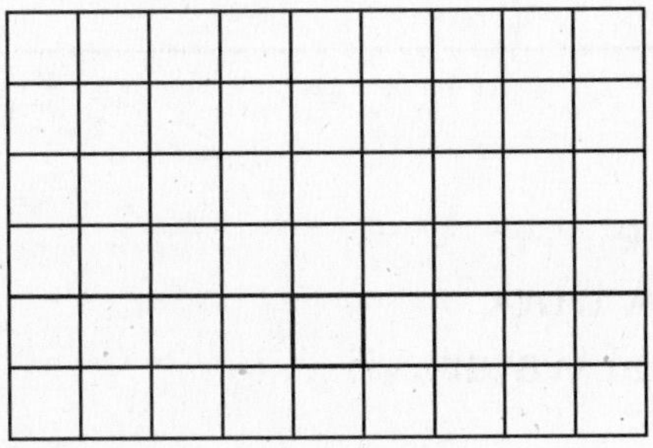

____ squares

12.
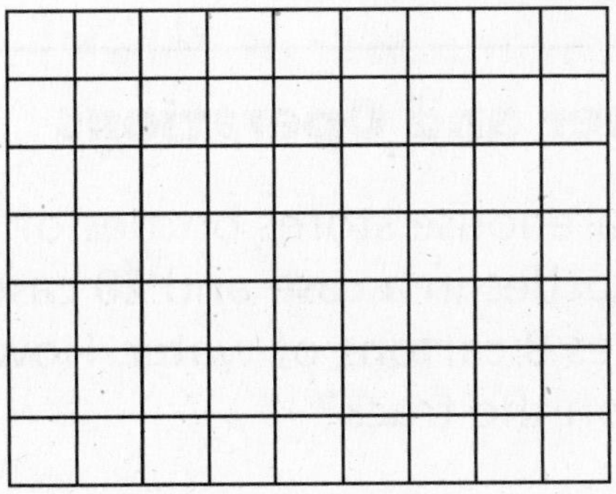

____ squares

Name ______________________________ Date ______________

Algebra

Write the rule that was used to find the output row. Then fill in any missing numbers.

1

Input	3	6	7	8	10	11	
Output	9	18	21	24	30		36

____

2

Input	8	12	20	24	30		42
Output	4		10		15	18	

____

Measurement

Write the time shown on each clock.

3

time: ________

4

time: ________

5

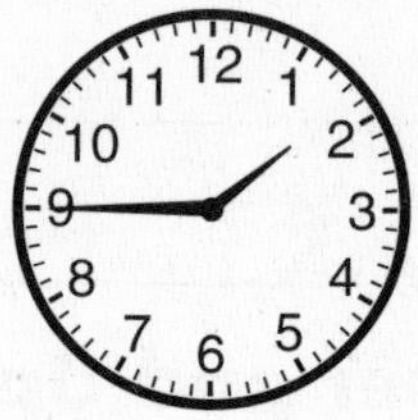

time: ________

Number and Operations

6 A warehouse stores bottles of water. There are 24 bottles in a case and 28 cases in a carton. A truck carries 8 cartons of water. How many bottles of water are on the truck?

________ bottles

Name ______________________ Date ____________

Spiral Review
Lesson 1

Geometry

Write the letters of the figures that are examples of the quadrilateral named.

1 Parallelogram

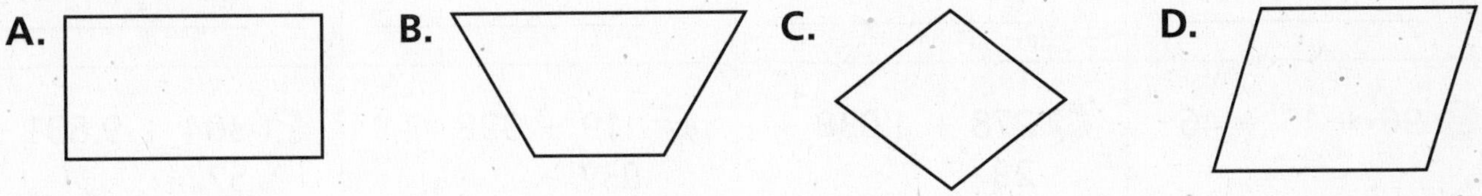

____

2 Rectangle

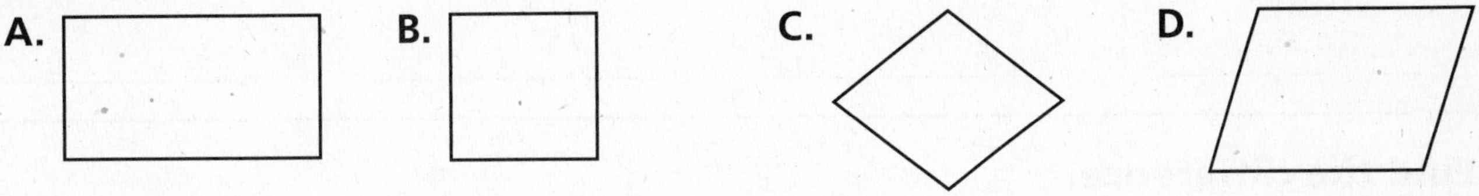

____

3 Rhombus

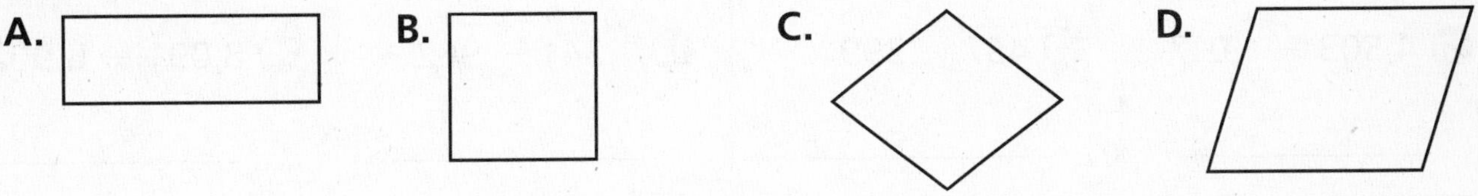

____

Measurement

Write the temperature shown on the thermometer.

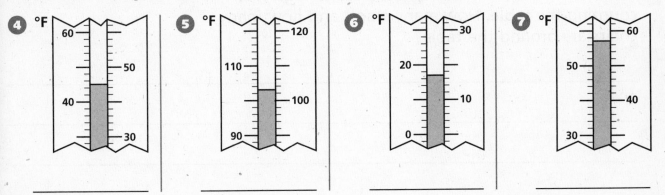

4 °F

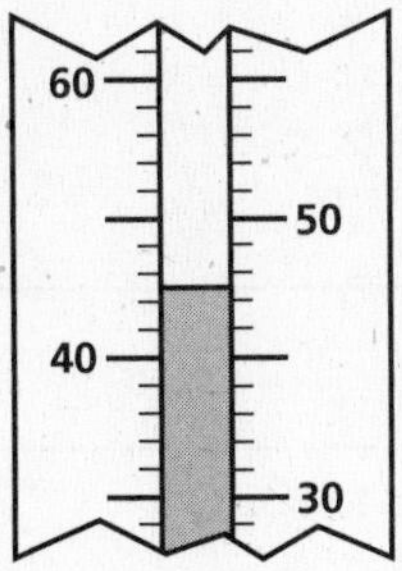

____

5 °F

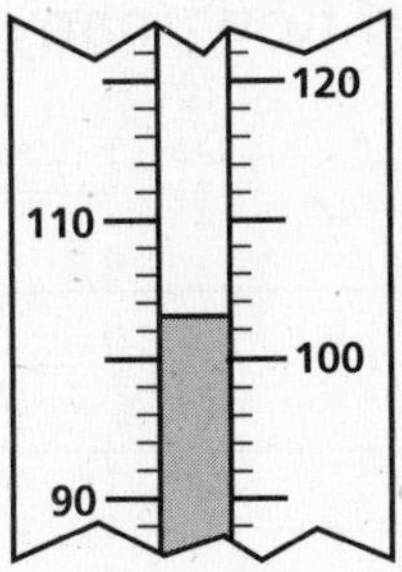

____

6 °F

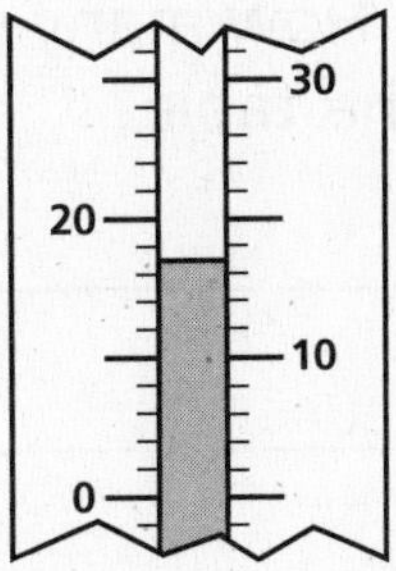

____

7 °F

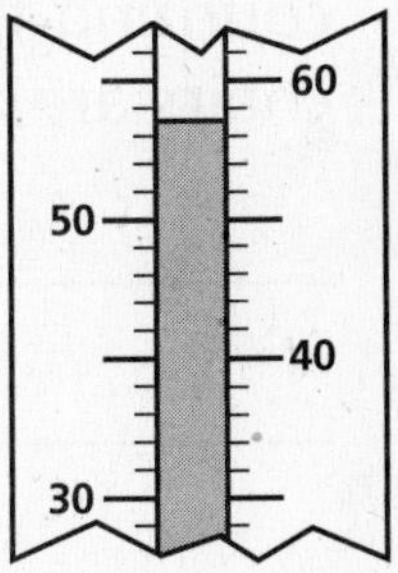

____

Name ______________________ Date ______________

Number and Operations

Find the sum.

1 670 + 186	2 184 + 72	3 340 + 298	4 817 + 309
5 96 + 15 + 46	6 278 + 1,038 + 29	7 119 + 398 + 937	8 304 + 9,831 + 572
9 103 + 2,349	10 2,406 + 1,058	11 459 + 6,793	12 994 + 8,713

Find the difference.

13 671 − 274	14 508 − 129	15 1,192 − 874	16 8,600 − 961
17 4,503 − 1,017	18 457 − 399	19 1,341 − 962	20 8,091 − 6,902

Problem Solving

Solve the problem. Explain your answer.

21 There are some 3-legged stools and some 4-legged chairs around a table. In all, there are 17 legs, not counting the table. How many stools and how many chairs are around the table?

Name ______________________ Date ______________

Spiral Review
Lesson 3

Algebra

Use patterns to complete each set of multiplication sentences.

1. $10 \times 9 = 90$
   $10 \times 90 =$ ______
   $10 \times 900 =$ ______

2. $10 \times 13 = 130$
   $10 \times 130 =$ ______
   $10 \times 1{,}300 =$ ______

3. $10 \times 19 = 190$
   $10 \times 190 =$ ______
   $10 \times 1{,}900 =$ ______

4. $10 \times 51 =$ ______
   $10 \times 510 =$ ______
   $10 \times 5{,}100 =$ ______

5. $10 \times 36 =$ ______
   $10 \times 360 =$ ______
   $10 \times 3{,}600 =$ ______

6. $10 \times 87 =$ ______
   $10 \times 870 =$ ______
   $10 \times 8{,}700 =$ ______

Geometry

Draw another rectangle that has the same perimeter but a different area. Use a separate sheet of paper for your drawings.

7. 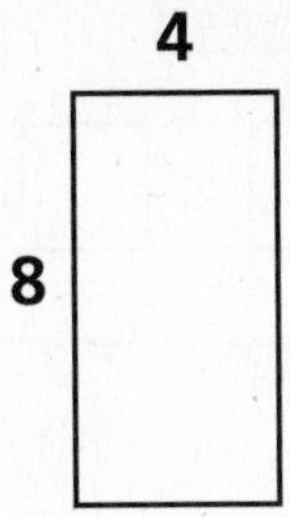

______

8. 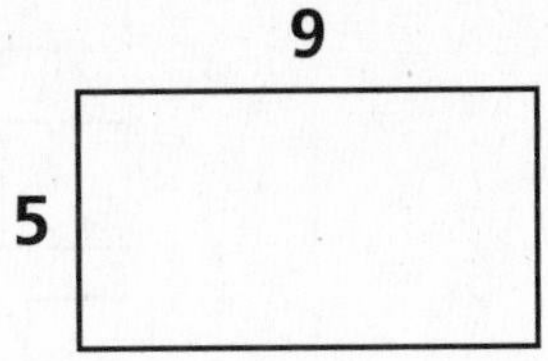

______

9. 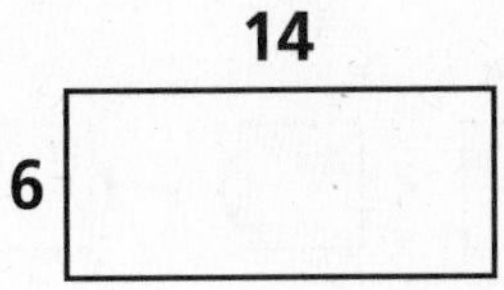

______

Draw another rectangle that has the same area but a different perimeter. Use a separate sheet of paper for your drawings.

10. 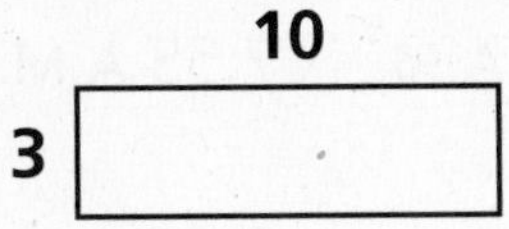

______

11. 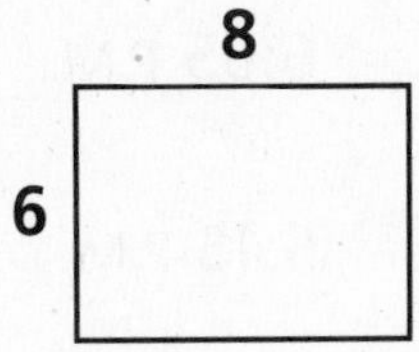

______

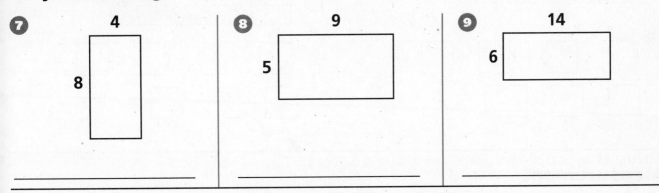

Name ____________________ Date ____________

Spiral Review
Lesson 4

Number and Operations

Complete the number sentence to name the total number of tiles in the array.

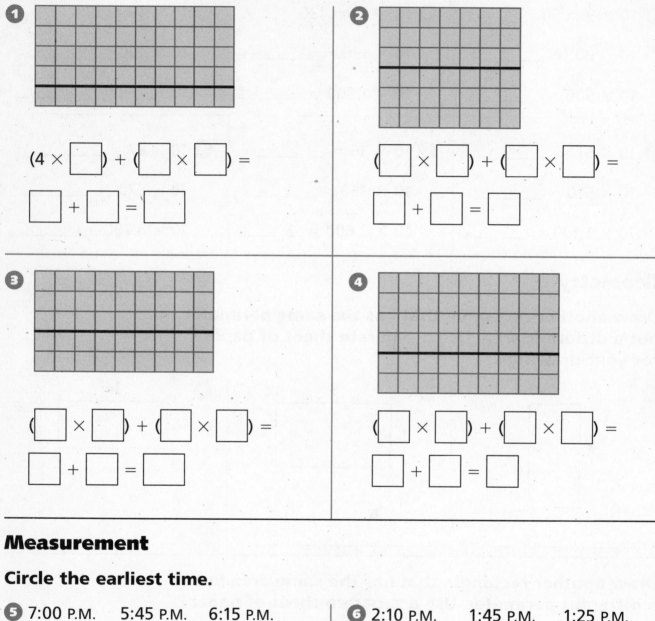

1. 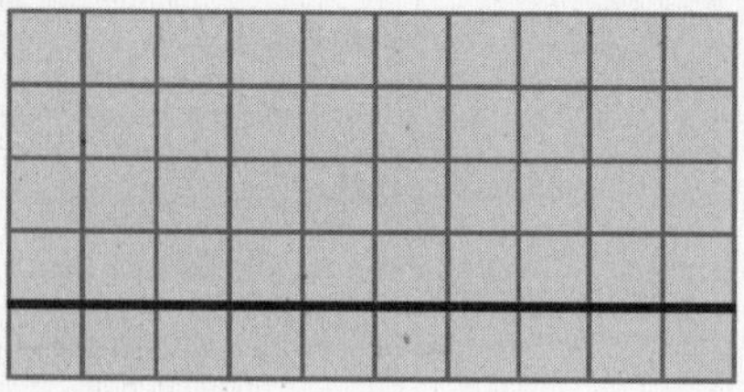

(4 × ☐) + (☐ × ☐) =

☐ + ☐ = ☐

2. 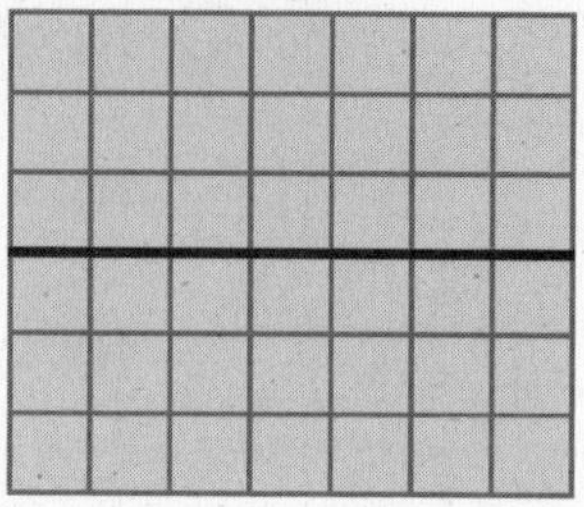

(☐ × ☐) + (☐ × ☐) =

☐ + ☐ = ☐

3. 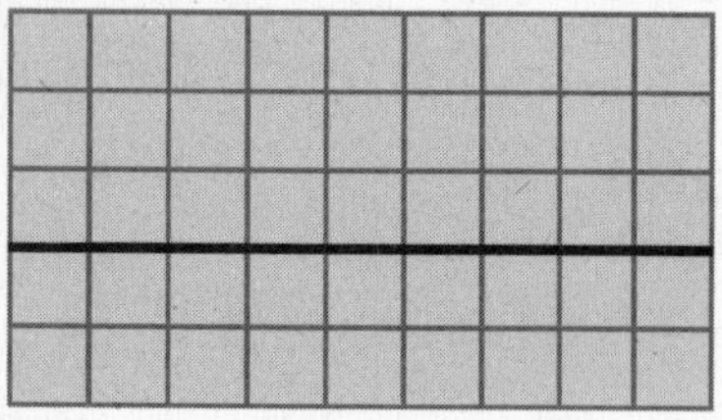

(☐ × ☐) + (☐ × ☐) =

☐ + ☐ = ☐

4. 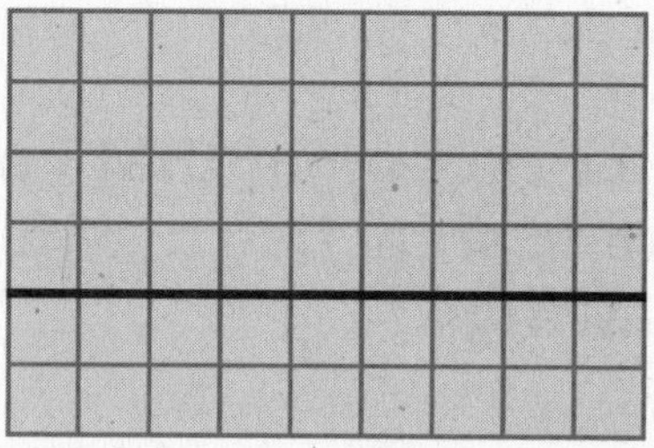

(☐ × ☐) + (☐ × ☐) =

☐ + ☐ = ☐

Measurement

Circle the earliest time.

5. 7:00 P.M. 5:45 P.M. 6:15 P.M.

6. 2:10 P.M. 1:45 P.M. 1:25 P.M.

7. 6:15 P.M. 5:55 P.M. 6:05 P.M.

8. 9:00 A.M. 8:15 A.M. 7:55 A.M.

9. 5:30 P.M. 5:20 P.M. 5:15 P.M.

10. 8:05 A.M. 7:40 A.M. 8:00 A.M.

Name ______________________ Date ____________

Spiral Review
Lesson 5

Data Analysis and Probability

For 1–3, use the pictograph.

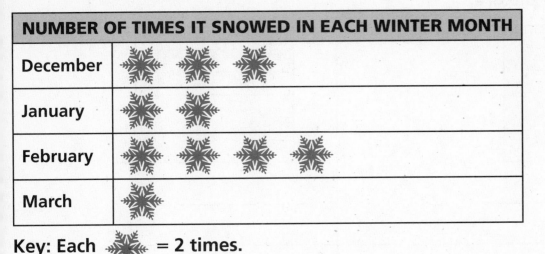

NUMBER OF TIMES IT SNOWED IN EACH WINTER MONTH	
December	
January	
February	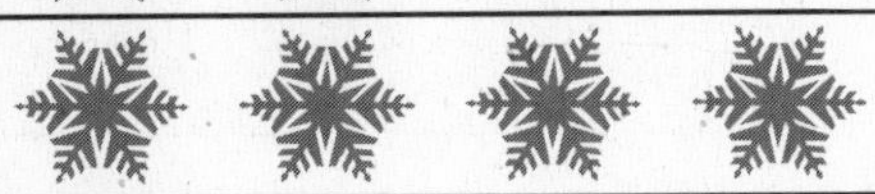
March	

Key: Each  **= 2 times.**

1. How many times did it snow during the four months? ________

2. Each time it snowed in December, there were 5 inches of snow. How many inches of snow were there in December? ________

3. It snowed a total of 24 inches in February. If there was the same amount of snow each time, how many inches did it snow each time in February? ________

Problem Solving

Solve the problem. Explain your answer.

4. The local bus stops near your house at 7:23 A.M., 7:39 A.M., 7:55 A.M., 8:11 A.M., and so on. If the pattern in the schedule continues, what is the earliest time you can get the bus at this stop after 8:30 A.M.?

____

____

____

Name ______________________ Date ______________

Algebra

Write a multiplication sentence to find the number of tiles in the picture.

1. 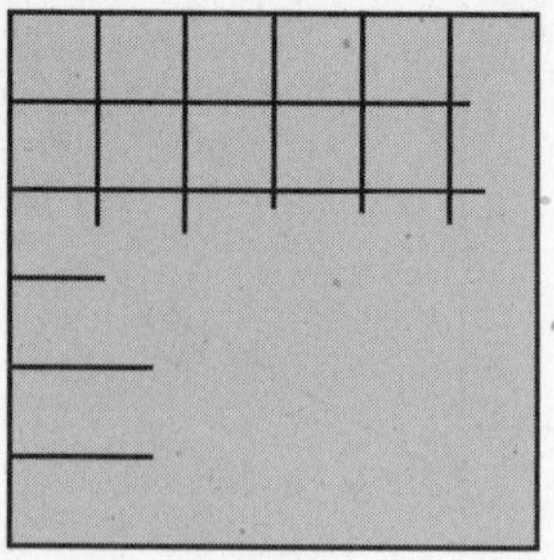

____

2. 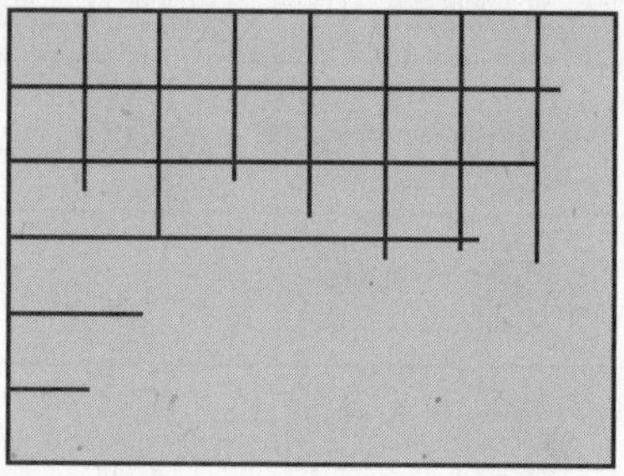

____

3. 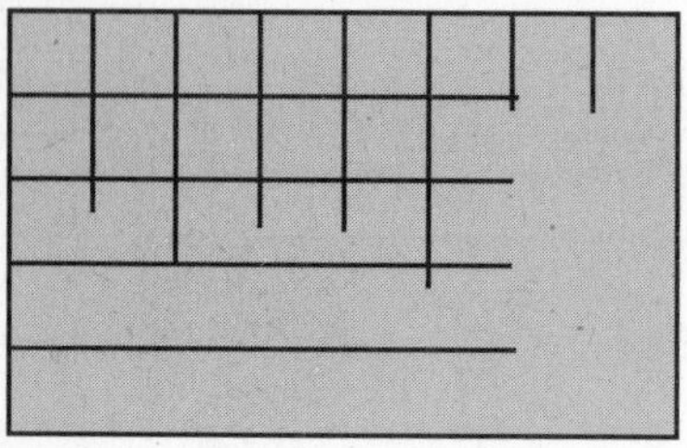

____

4. 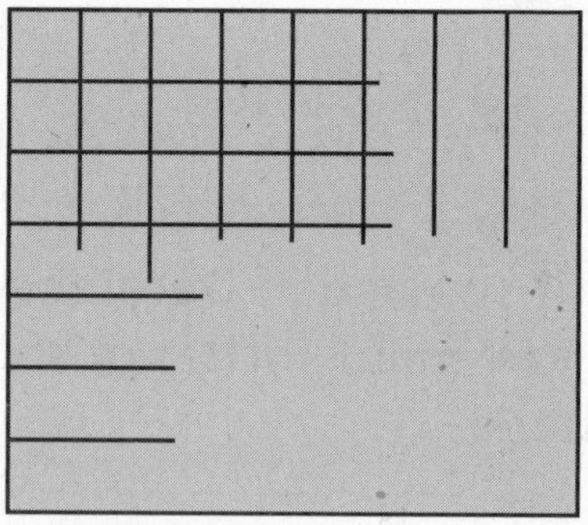

____

Problem Solving

Solve the problem. Explain your answer.

5. You can fill the pool from a hose that pours 10 gallons per minute. If the pool holds 3,000 gallons of water, how many hours will it take to fill?

____

____

____

Name ______________________ Date ____________

Spiral Review
Lesson 7

Geometry

Estimate the perimeter of each rectangle. Use only whole numbers in your estimates.

1.
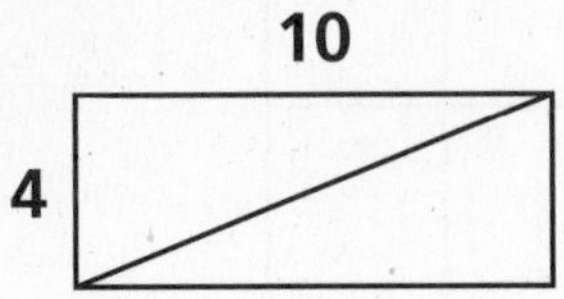

____

2.
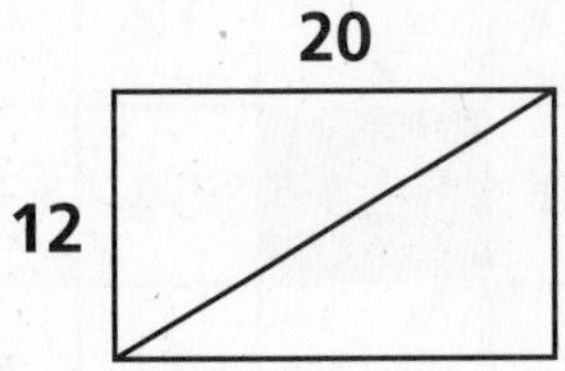

____

3.
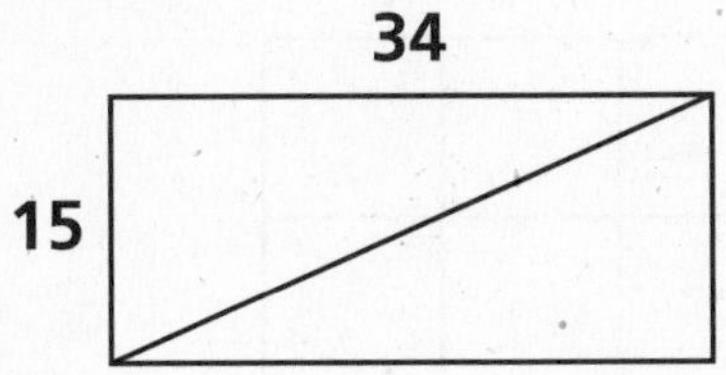

____

4.
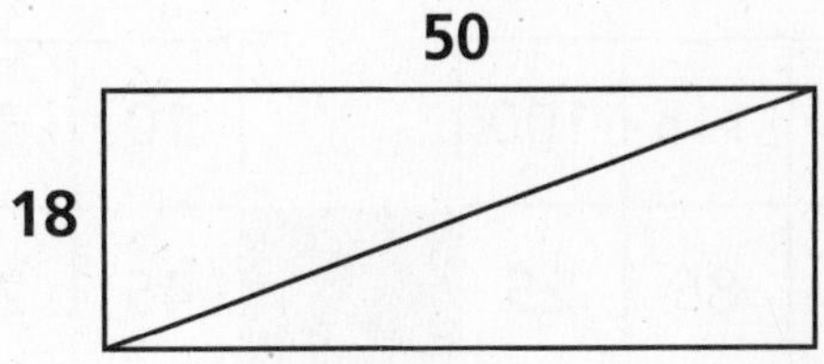

____

Reasoning and Proof

For 5–8, use the graph.

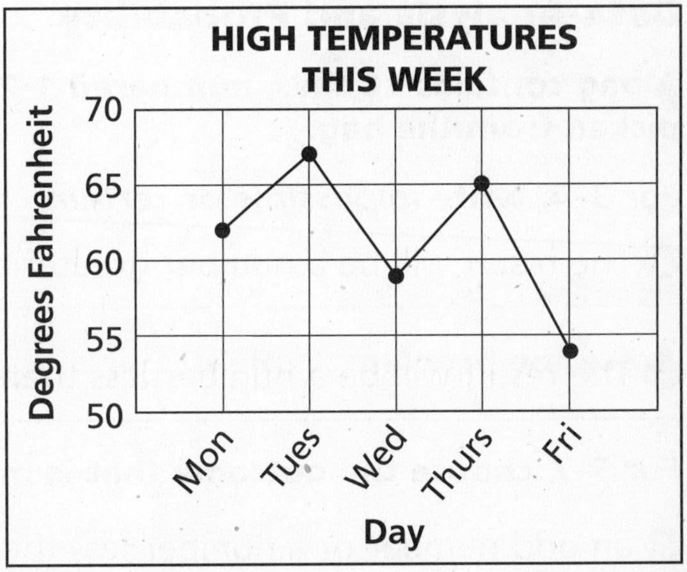

5. On how many days was the high temperature below 60°F?

____

6. On how many days was the high temperature above 65°F?

____

7. Estimate the range of high temperatures (the difference between the highest and lowest).

____

8. What is a reasonable high temperature for Saturday?

____

Name ______________________ Date ____________

Spiral Review
Lesson 8

Number and Operations

Subtract the magic squares.

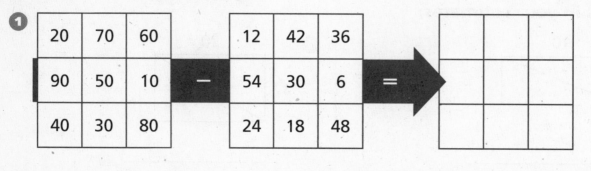

1.

20	70	60
90	50	10
40	30	80

−

12	42	36
54	30	6
24	18	48

=

2.

40	115	100
145	85	25
70	55	130

−

10	35	30
45	25	5
20	15	40

=

Data Analysis and Probability

A bag contains 20 tiles, numbered 1–20. One tile is picked from the bag.

For 3–4, write *impossible* or *certain.*

3. The result will be a number greater than 20. ____________

4. The result will be a number less than 40. ____________

For 5–7, choose the outcome that is more likely.

5. an odd number or a number less than 7 ____________

6. a factor of 4 or a multiple of 4 ____________

7. a one-digit number or a two-digit number ____________

Geometry

Answer these questions about transformations of Triangle A.

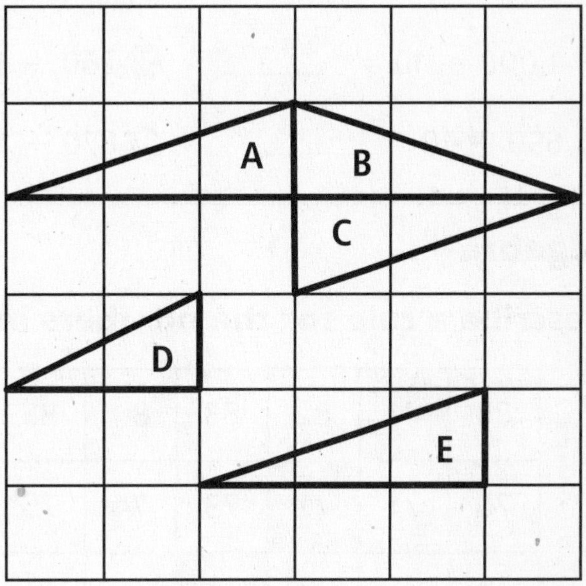

1. Which triangle is a translation of Triangle A?

   Triangle ________

2. Which triangle is a reflection of Triangle A?

   Triangle ________

3. Which triangle is a rotation of Triangle A?

   Triangle ________

Problem Solving

Solve the problem. Explain your answer.

4. Kerry had $8 when she came back from the store. She bought a CD for $10 and two DVDs for $15 each. How much did she have before she went shopping? ________

5. Ms. Johnson gives out pencils to her students. She has 12 left. There are 23 students in her class, and each student gets 2 pencils. How many pencils did she have to begin with? ________

Name ______________________ Date ______________

Number and Operations

Write the quotient.

1. 80 ÷ 10 = ________
2. 120 ÷ 10 = ________
3. 210 ÷ 10 = ________
4. 1,000 ÷ 10 = ________
5. 260 ÷ 10 = ________
6. 1,100 ÷ 10 = ________
7. 690 ÷ 10 = ________
8. 870 ÷ 10 = ________
9. 2,320 ÷ 10 = ________

Algebra

Describe a rule for the numbers in the shaded boxes.

10.

80	81	82	83	84	85	86	87	88	89
70	71	72	73	74	75	76	77	78	79
60	61	62	63	64	65	66	67	68	69

11.

30	31	32	33	34	35	36	37	38	39
20	21	22	23	24	25	26	27	28	29
10	11	12	13	14	15	16	17	18	19

Geometry

Name the type of angle indicated by the letter. Choose from *right angle, acute angle,* or *obtuse angle.*

12. 13. 14.

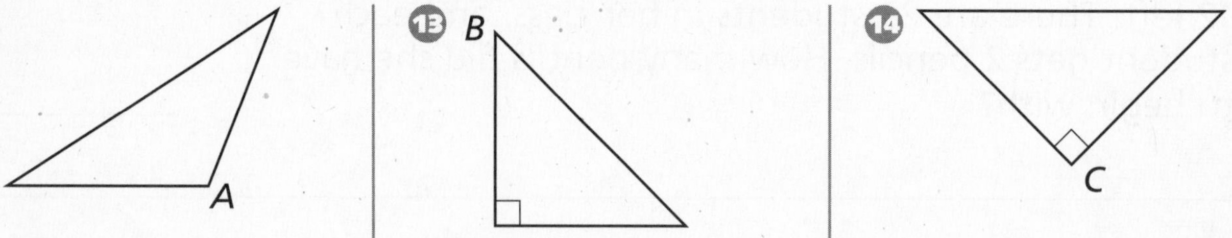

________ ________ ________

Name ______________________________ Date ______________

Data Analysis and Probability

For Problems 1–4, use the table and bar graph below.

FAVORITE SCHOOL DAY	
School Day	Number of Student Votes
Monday	4 votes
Tuesday	7 votes
Wednesday	6 votes
Thursday	3 votes
Friday	11 votes

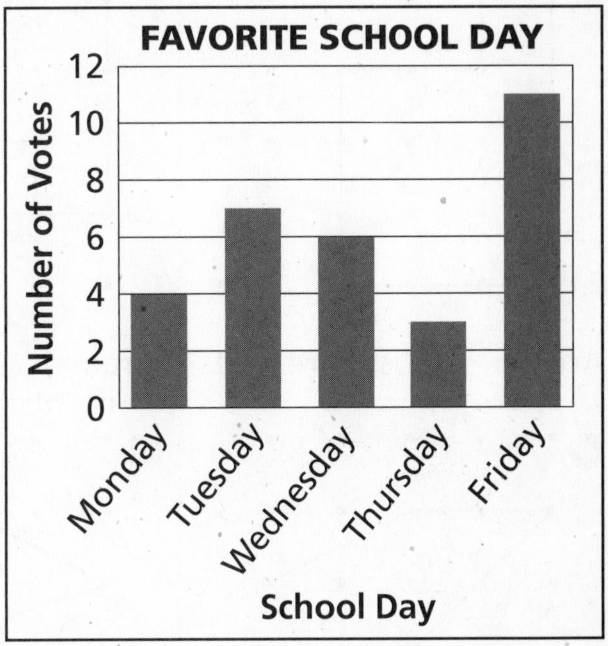

1. Do both displays show the same data? Explain.

____

____

2. If each student voted once, how many students voted in all?

____

3. What is the difference in the number of votes between the day with the most votes and the day with the fewest votes?

____

Problem Solving

Solve the problem. Explain your answer.

4. Jack's dog weighs 5 pounds more than his cat. Together, the pets weigh 41 pounds. How much does the dog weigh?

____

____

____

Name ______________________ Date ______________

Measurement

Find the area of each figure.

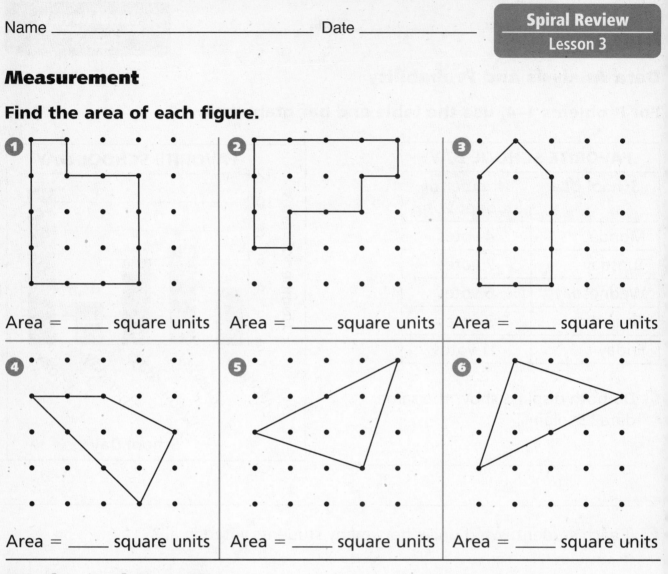

1. 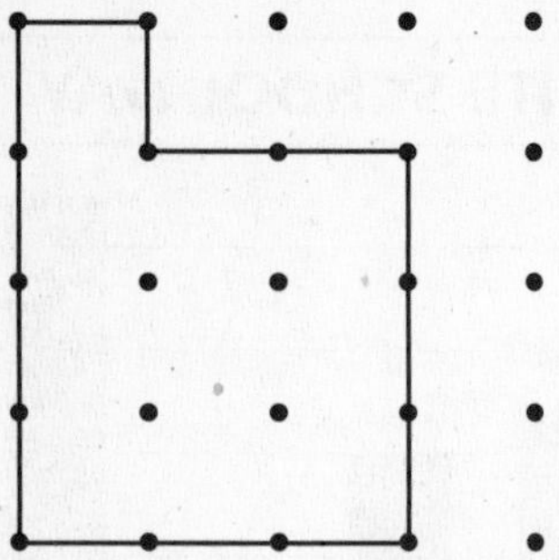

Area = ____ square units

2. 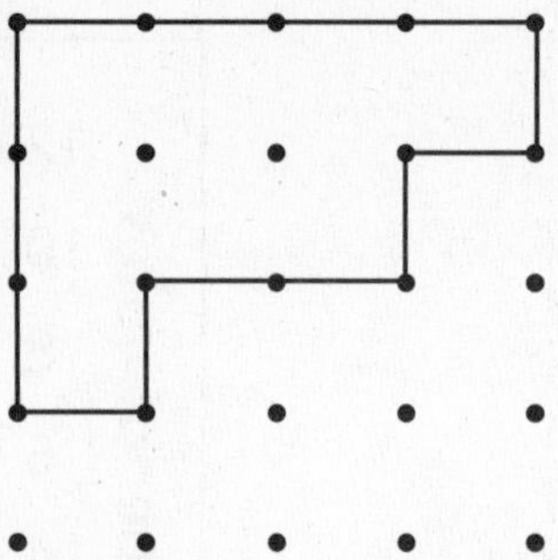

Area = ____ square units

3. 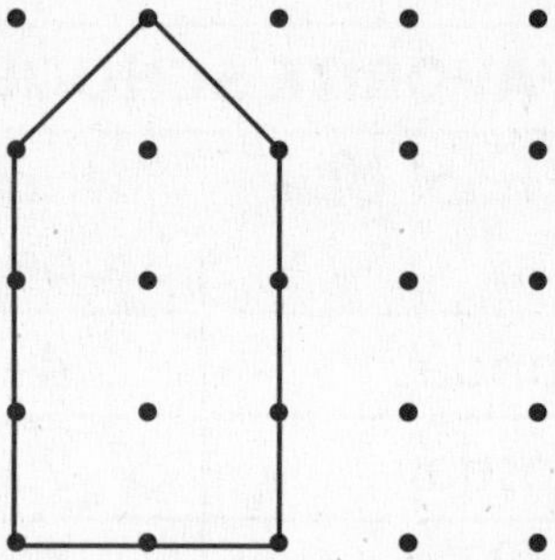

Area = ____ square units

4. 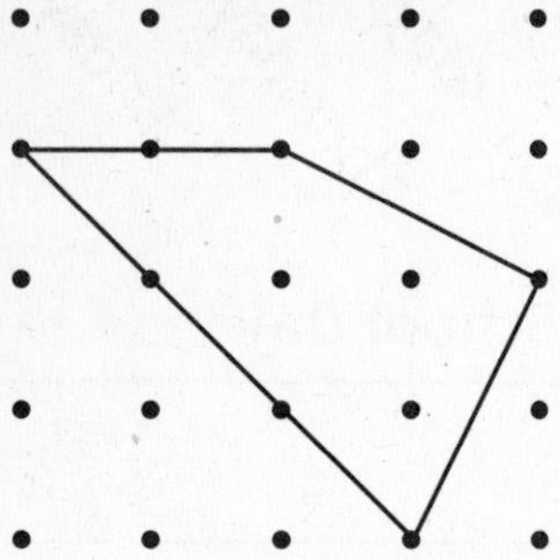

Area = ____ square units

5. 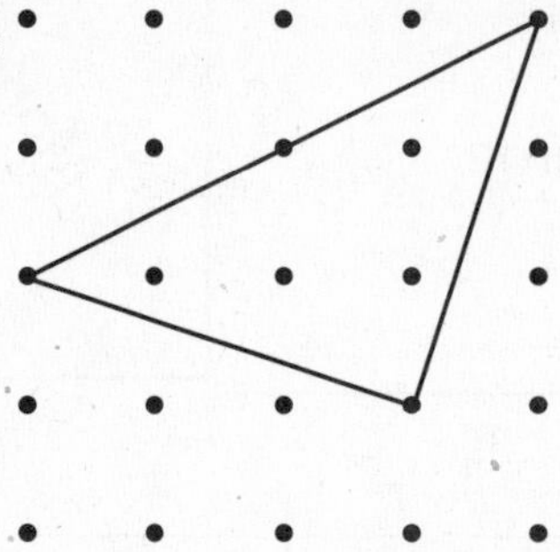

Area = ____ square units

6. 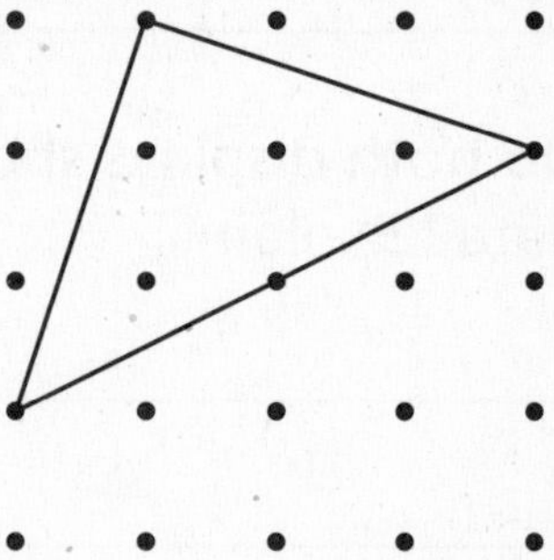

Area = ____ square units

Number and Operations

Write the fact family that is shown by each array.

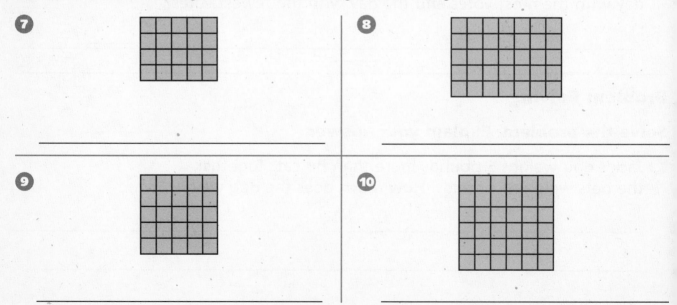

7. 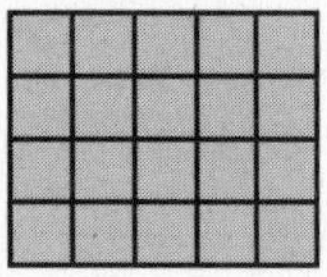

____

8. 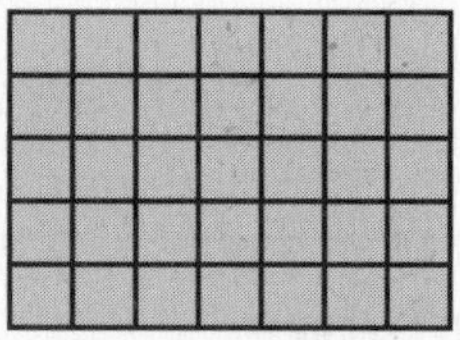

____

9. 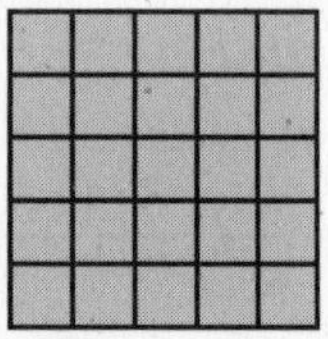

____

10. 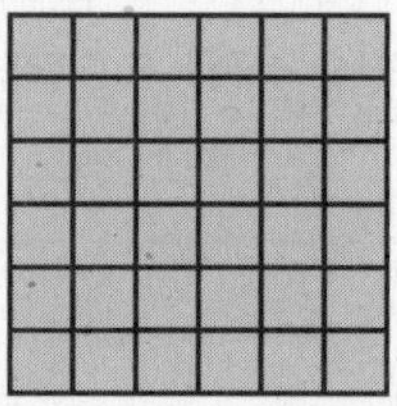

____

Name ______________________________ Date ______________

Algebra

Use a pattern to complete each multiplication table. Then complete the difference table.

1

×	3	4
1	3	4
2		
3		

Difference
1

2

×	6	7
1		
2		
3		

Difference

3

×	5	6
1		
2		
3		

Difference

4

×	3	5
1		
2		
3		

Difference

Geometry

Write a specific name to identify each figure. Then write the number of lines of symmetry in each figure.

5

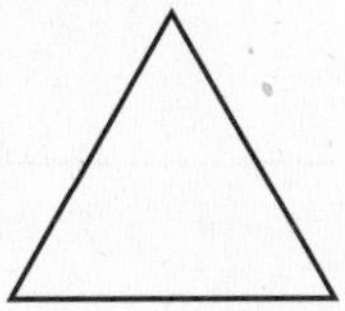

____

6

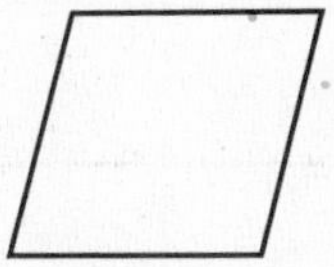

____

7

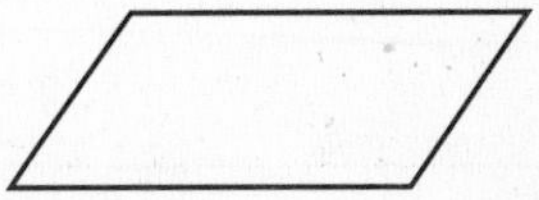

____

8

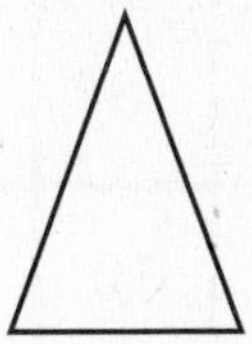

____

9

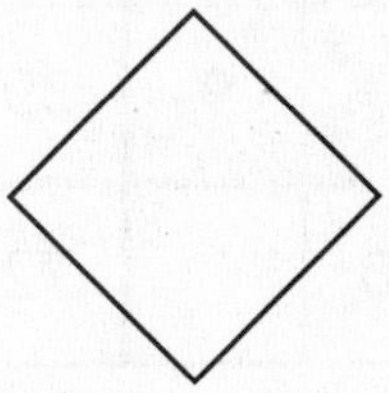

____

10

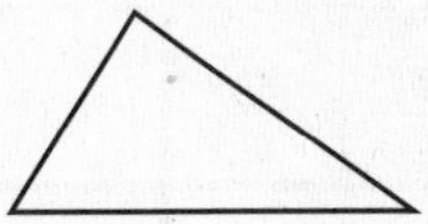

____

Name ______________________ Date ____________

Spiral Review
Lesson 5

Number and Operations

Shade the tiles to show the division.

1. 23 ÷ 6 = 3 r5

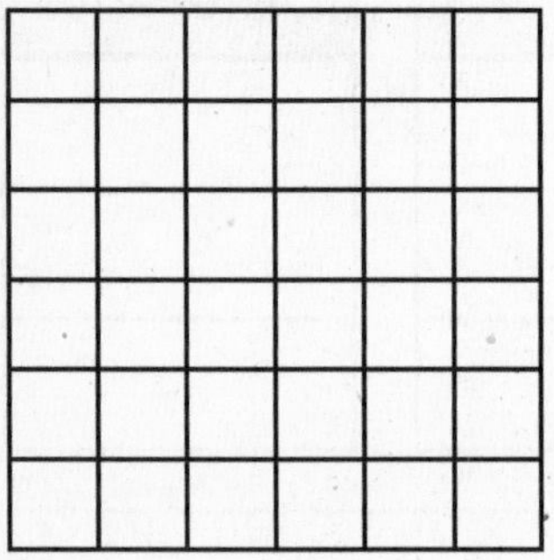

2. 38 ÷ 5 = 7 r3

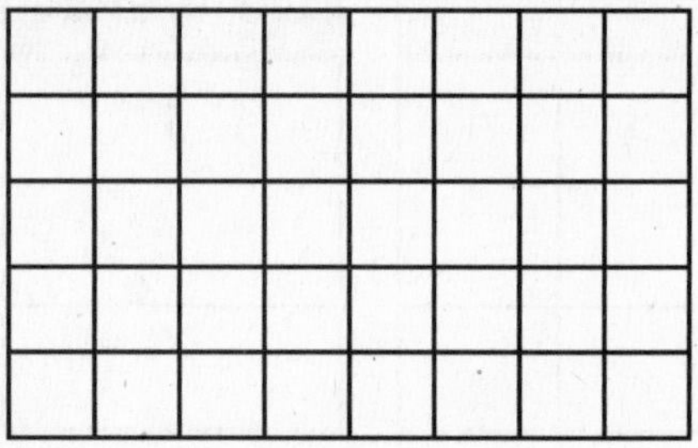

Problem Solving

Solve the problem. Explain your answer.

3. A truck made a delivery of 32 pies to each of 9 bakeries. How many pies were delivered in all? Show how you got your answer.

____

____

Reasoning and Proof

Complete each puzzle.

4.

30	3	33
80	7	
110	10	

5.

	3	
	9	39
60		72

6.

60		62
	8	
110	10	

Name ______________________ Date ____________

Spiral Review
Lesson 6

Number and Operations

Write fractions to name the shaded and unshaded parts.

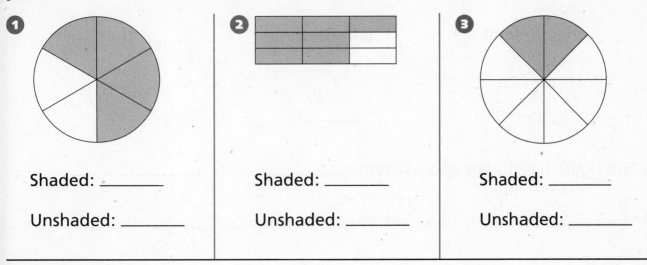

1. 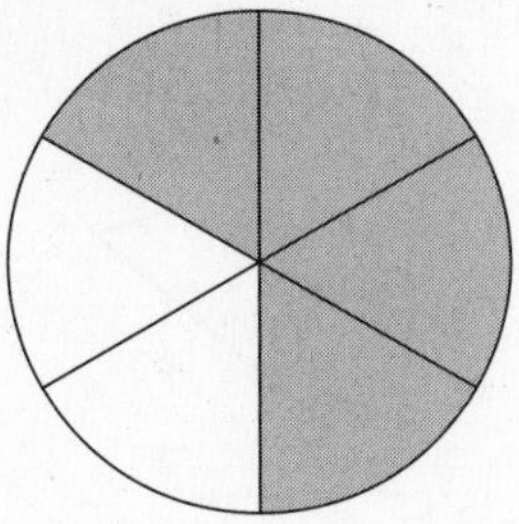

Shaded: ______

Unshaded: ______

2. 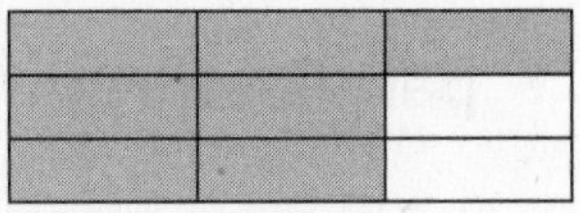

Shaded: ______

Unshaded: ______

3. 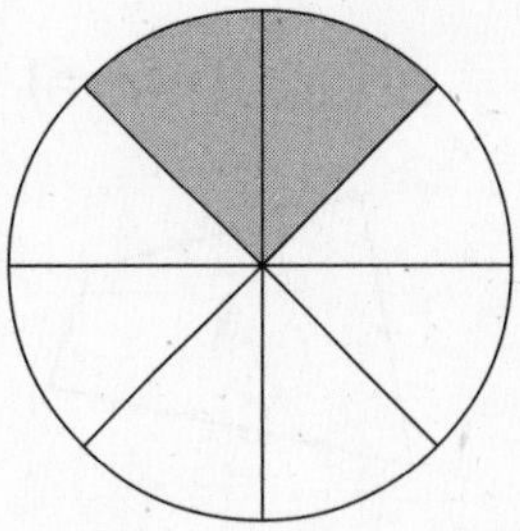

Shaded: ______

Unshaded: ______

Measurement

Circle the more reasonable weight.

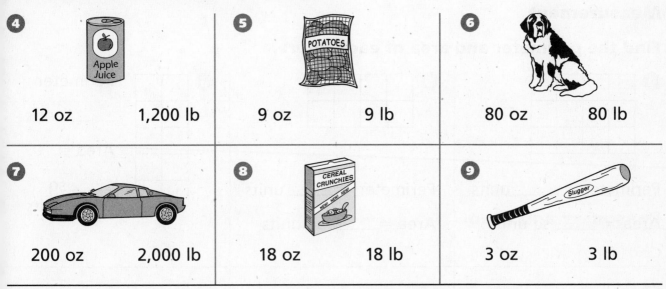

4. 

12 oz   1,200 lb

5. 

9 oz   9 lb

6. 

80 oz   80 lb

7. 

200 oz   2,000 lb

8. 

18 oz   18 lb

9. 

3 oz   3 lb

Problem Solving

Choose a number that makes sense. Solve the problem.

10. Thomas walks ______ to school each day. He walks the same number of blocks home. How many blocks does he walk in 5 days?

____

Name ______________________ Date ____________

Spiral Review
Lesson 7

Geometry

Find the figure(s) des each statement below. Write the letter(s).

quadrilateral **parallelogram** **trapezoid**

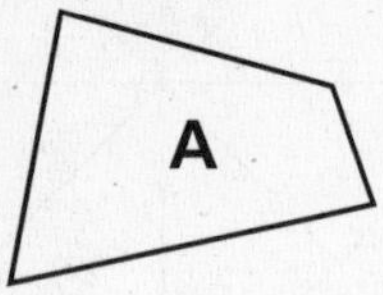

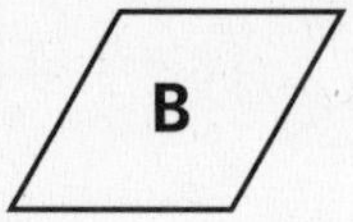

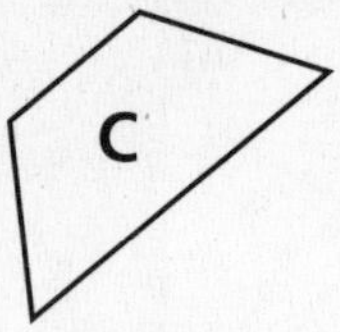

1. The figure has 4 sides and is closed. ____________

2. The figure has exactly two pairs of parallel sides. ____________

3. The figure has exactly one pair of parallel sides. ____________

Measurement

Find the perimeter and area of each figure.

4. 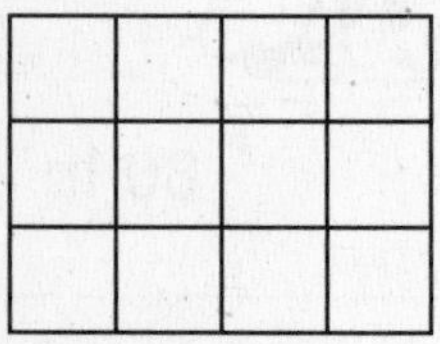

Perimeter = _____ units

Area = _____ sq units

5. 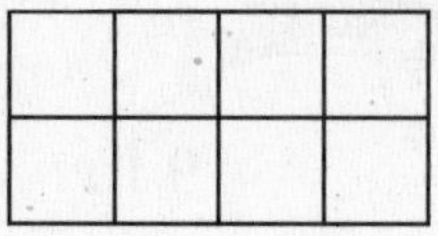

Perimeter = _____ units

Area = _____ sq units

6. 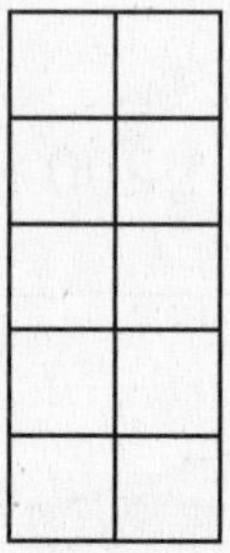

Perimeter = _____ units

Area = _____ sq units

7. 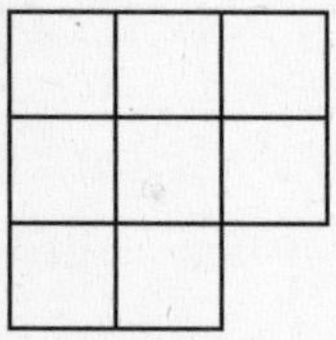

Perimeter = _____ units

Area = _____ sq units

8. 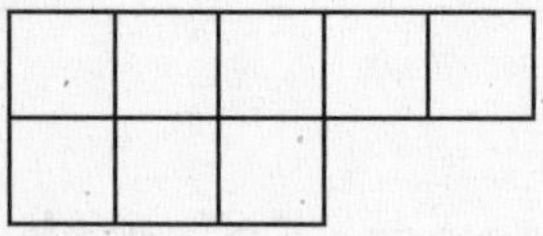

Perimeter = _____ units

Area = _____ sq units

9. 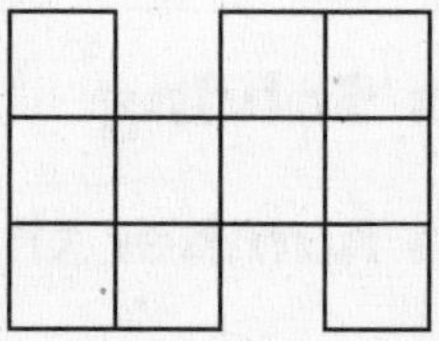

Perimeter = _____ units

Area = _____ sq units

Name ______________________ Date ____________

Spiral Review
Lesson 8

Algebra

Complete each table. Then write a rule.

1.

INPUT	4	5	8	13
OUTPUT	7	8	11	

Rule: ______________________

2.

INPUT	3	6		14	18
OUTPUT	6	12	18		36

Rule: ______________________

Data Analysis and Probability

Write *yes* or *no* to tell whether the spinner is fair for the game described. Explain.

3. Game: Player A wins if the spinner lands on a number less than 4. Player B wins if the spinner lands on any other number.

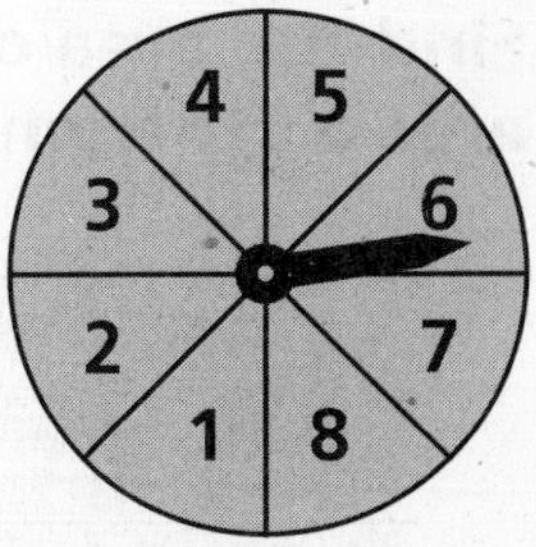

____

____

____

Reasoning and Proof

Use place value to add.

4. 327 = 300 + 20 + 7
+152 = 100 + 50 + 2

= 400 + ______ + ______

= ______

5. 738 = ______ + ______ + ______

+373 = ______ + ______ + ______

= ______ + ______ + ______

= ______

Name ______________________ Date ____________

Geometry

Name the triangle(s) described by each statement. Write the letter(s).

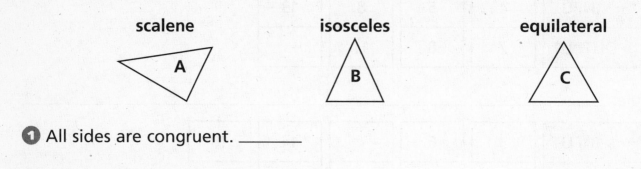

scalene

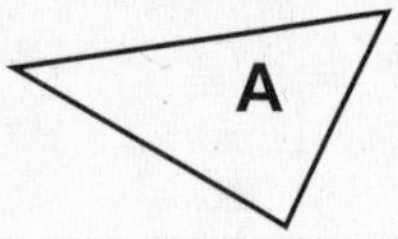

isosceles

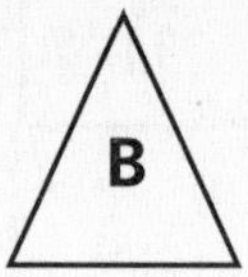

equilateral

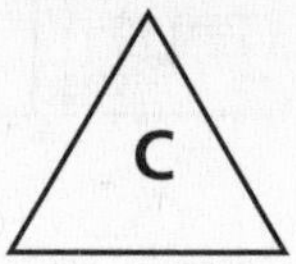

1. All sides are congruent. ________

2. The triangle has 3 angles. ________

3. There is at least one pair of congruent sides. ________

Problem Solving

Find the area of each smaller part. Then find the area of the whole figure.

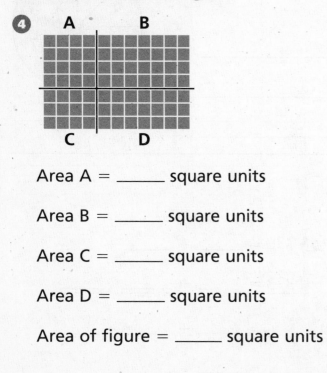

4.

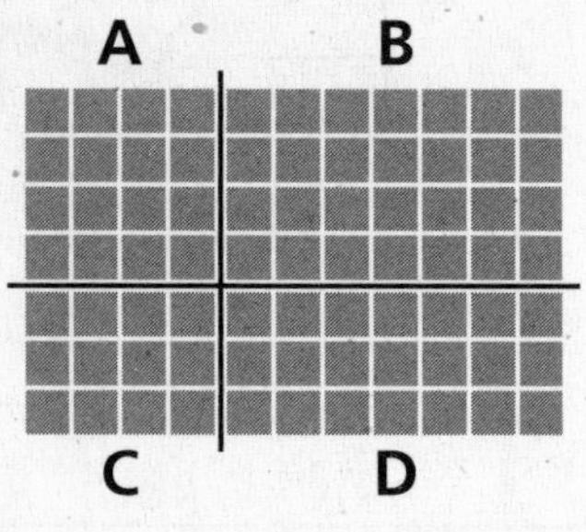

Area A = ______ square units

Area B = ______ square units

Area C = ______ square units

Area D = ______ square units

Area of figure = ______ square units

5.

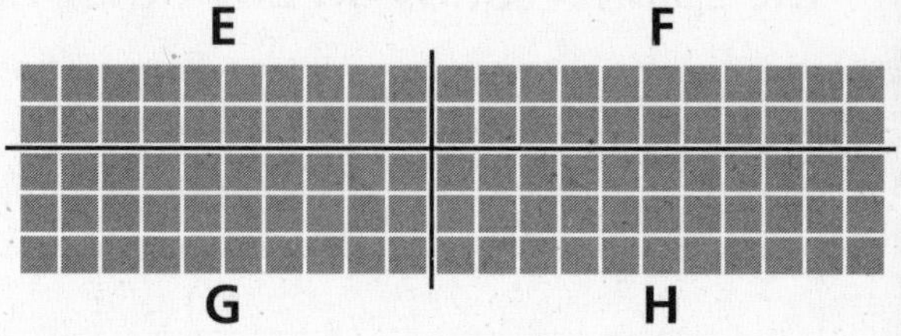

Area E = ______ square units

Area F = ______ square units

Area G = ______ square units

Area H = ______ square units

Area of figure = ______ square units

Name ______________________ Date ______________

Spiral Review
Lesson 10

Number and Operations

For Problems 1–5, find the value.

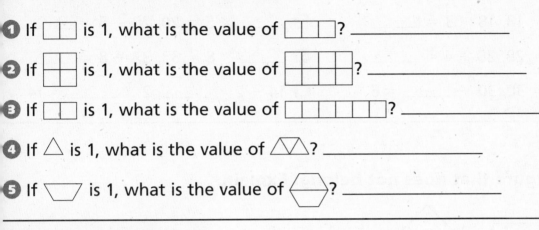

1. If 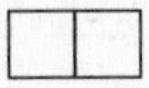 is 1, what is the value of 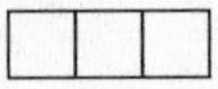? ______________

2. If 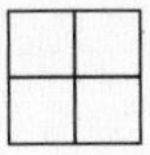 is 1, what is the value of 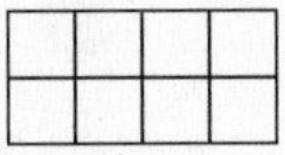? ______________

3. If 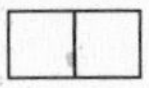 is 1, what is the value of 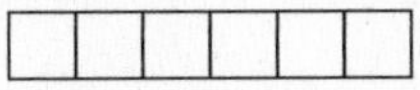? ______________

4. If  is 1, what is the value of 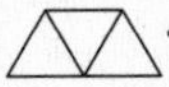? ______________

5. If 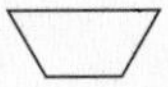 is 1, what is the value of 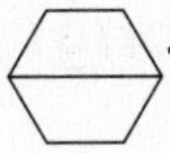? ______________

Reasoning and Proof

Solve each puzzle.

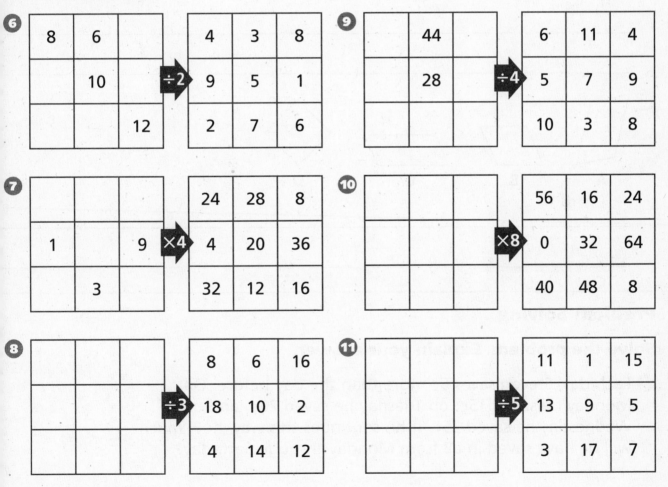

6.

8	6	
	10	
		12

÷2 →

4	3	8
9	5	1
2	7	6

9.

	44	
	28	

÷4 →

6	11	4
5	7	9
10	3	8

7.

1		9
	3	

×4 →

24	28	8
4	20	36
32	12	16

10.

×8 →

56	16	24
0	32	64
40	48	8

8.

÷3 →

8	6	16
18	10	2
4	14	12

11.

÷5 →

11	1	15
13	9	5
3	17	7

Name ______________________ Date ______________

Algebra

Find the missing numbers.

1. 3 × ______ = 18, 18 ÷ 3 = ______
2. ______ × 5 = 20, 20 ÷ 5 = ______
3. 4 × ______ = 28, 28 ÷ 4 = ______
4. ______ × 8 = 32, 32 ÷ 8 = ______
5. ______ × 6 = 30, 30 ÷ ______ = 6
6. 14 ÷ 2 = ______, 2 × ______ = 14

Geometry

Choose the figure that does not belong. Explain.

7.

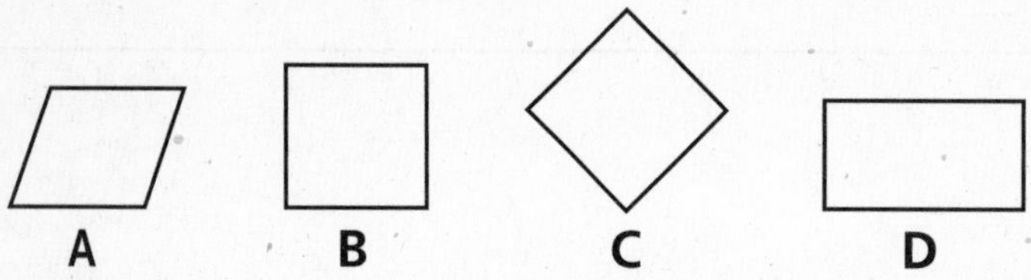

____

____

8.

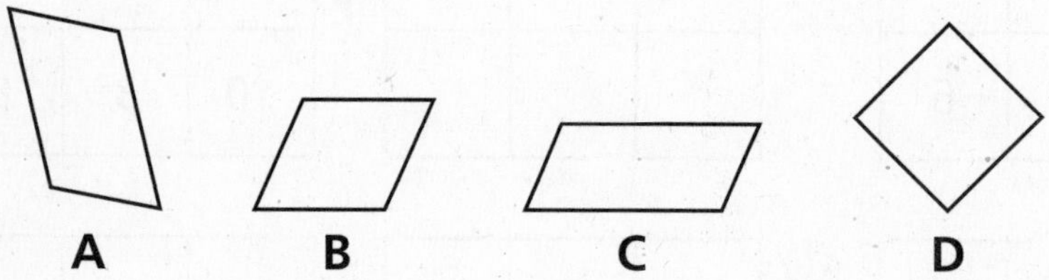

____

____

Problem Solving

Solve the problem. Explain your answer.

9. Each day, Steven saves 5¢ more than the day before. On Monday he saved 15¢, on Tuesday he saved 20¢, and on Wednesday he saved 25¢. If he continues this way, how much will he have saved in all from Monday through Saturday?

____

Name ________________________ Date ____________

Spiral Review
Lesson 1

Number and Operations

Add the magic squares. Write the sum for the new square.

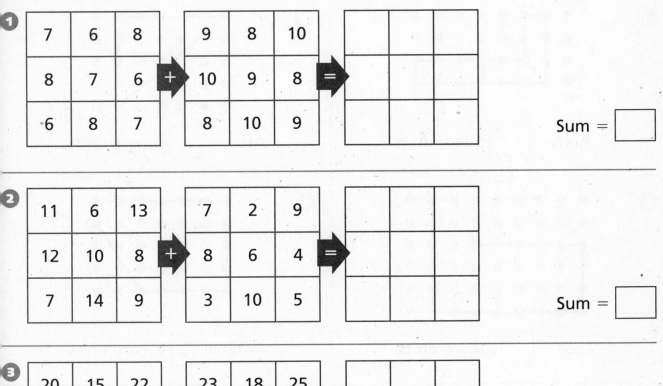

1

7	6	8
8	7	6
6	8	7

+

9	8	10
10	9	8
8	10	9

=

Sum = ____

2

11	6	13
12	10	8
7	14	9

+

7	2	9
8	6	4
3	10	5

=

Sum = ____

3

20	15	22
21	19	17
16	23	18

+

23	18	25
24	22	20
19	26	21

=

Sum = ____

Problem Solving

Solve the problem. Explain your answer.

4 Planes are arriving at an airport every 8 minutes. A plane has arrived at 5:13 P.M. At what time will the last plane before 6:00 P.M. arrive?

____

____

____

Name ______________________ Date ____________

Spiral Review
Lesson 2

Geometry

Find the area of the figure. The smallest square on the grid has an area of 1 square unit.

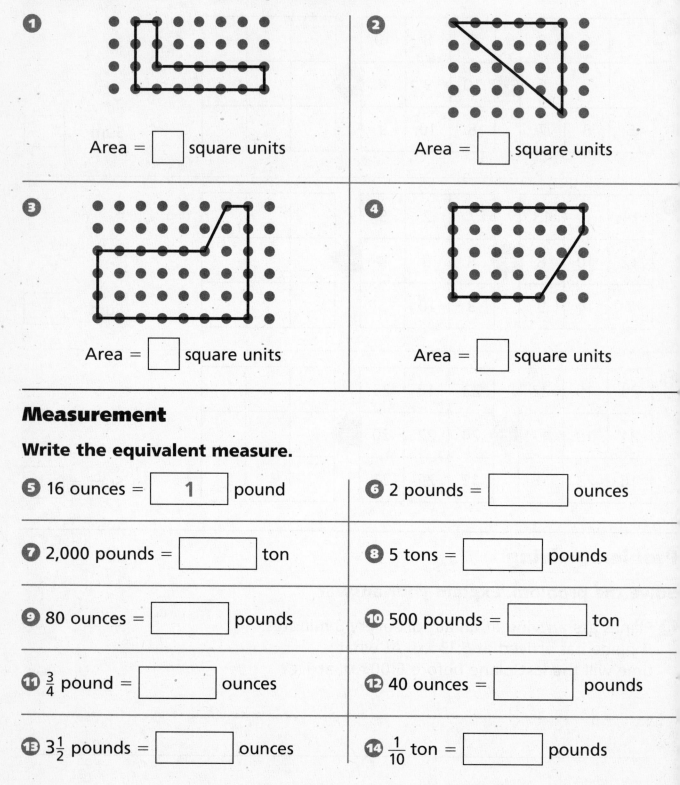

1. 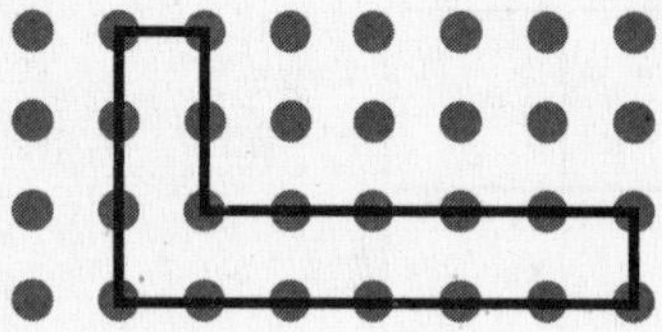

Area = ☐ square units

2. 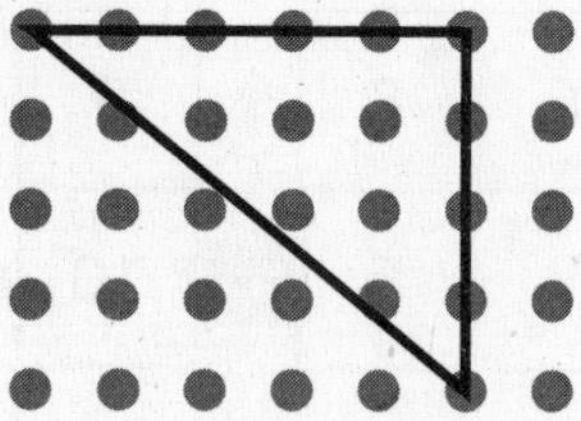

Area = ☐ square units

3. 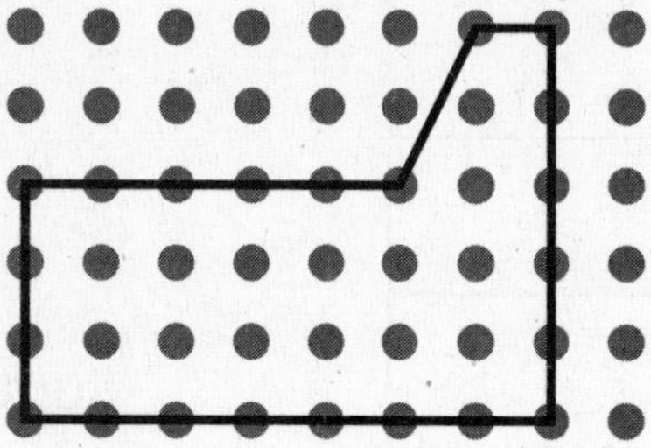

Area = ☐ square units

4. 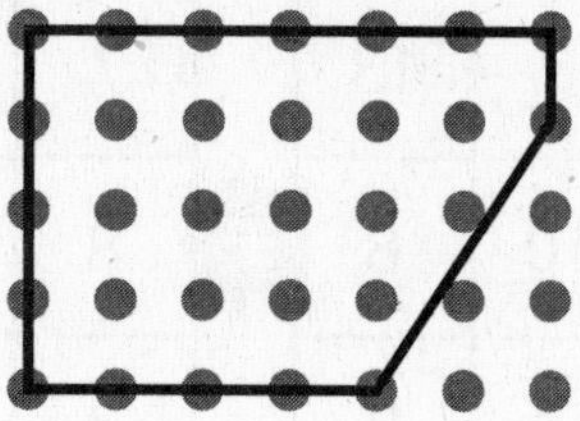

Area = ☐ square units

Measurement

Write the equivalent measure.

5. 16 ounces = 1 pound

6. 2 pounds = ☐ ounces

7. 2,000 pounds = ☐ ton

8. 5 tons = ☐ pounds

9. 80 ounces = ☐ pounds

10. 500 pounds = ☐ ton

11. $\frac{3}{4}$ pound = ☐ ounces

12. 40 ounces = ☐ pounds

13. $3\frac{1}{2}$ pounds = ☐ ounces

14. $\frac{1}{10}$ ton = ☐ pounds

Name ______________________________ Date ______________

Spiral Review
Lesson 3

Number and Operations

Complete the multiplication sentences for the picture.

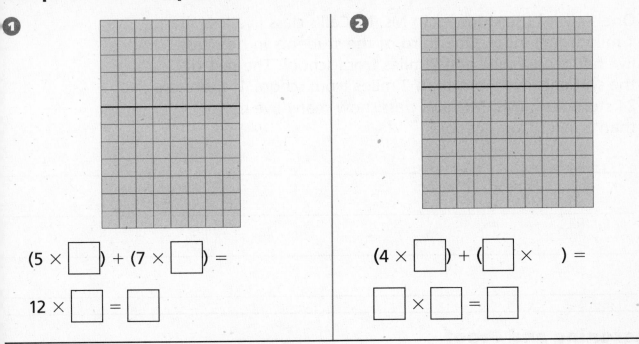

1.

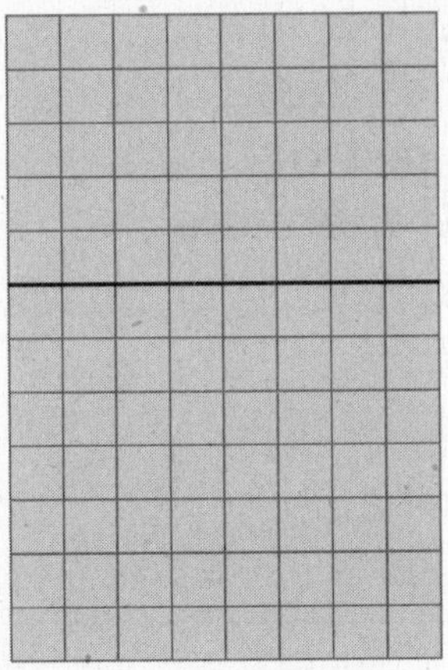

(5 × ___) + (7 × ___) =

12 × ___ = ___

2.

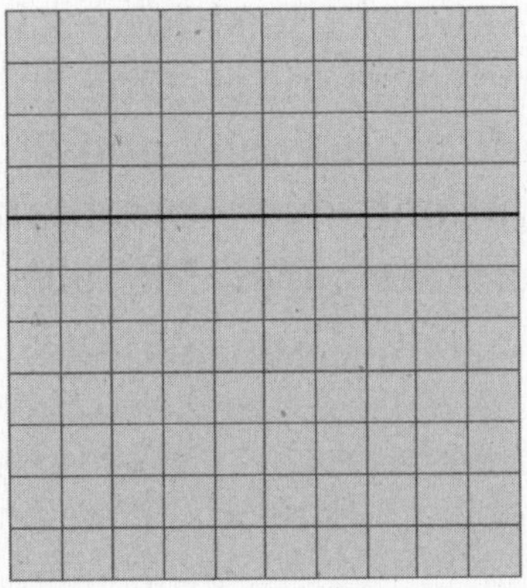

(4 × ___) + (___ ×) =

___ × ___ = ___

Data Analysis and Probability

For 3–6, use the spinners. List all possible outcomes for the experiment.

Spinner A

Spinner B

3. You spin Spinner A once.

____

____

4. You spin Spinner B once.

____

____

5. You spin Spinner A once. Then you spin it again and add the two results.

____

____

6. You spin both spinners. Then you subtract the smaller number from the greater number.

____

Name ______________________________ Date ____________

Problem Solving

Solve the problem. Explain your answer.

1. One sixth of the students in Ms. McCall's class live less than 1 mile from school. One third of the students in her class live between 1 mile and 2 miles from school. The rest of the students live more than 2 miles from school. If there are 24 students in Ms. McCall's class, how many live more than 2 miles from school?

____

____

____

____

Reasoning and Proof

Work backward to complete the magic squares.

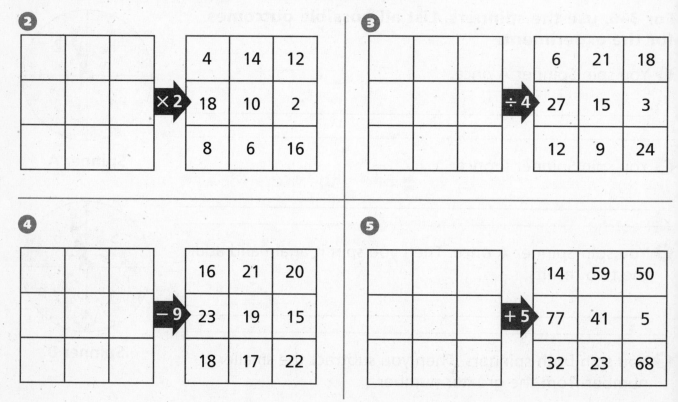

2.

→ × 2 →

4	14	12
18	10	2
8	6	16

3.

→ ÷ 4 →

6	21	18
27	15	3
12	9	24

4.

→ − 9 →

16	21	20
23	19	15
18	17	22

5.

→ + 5 →

14	59	50
77	41	5
32	23	68

Name ____________________ Date ____________

Geometry

Write whether the triangle is *acute, obtuse,* or *right.*

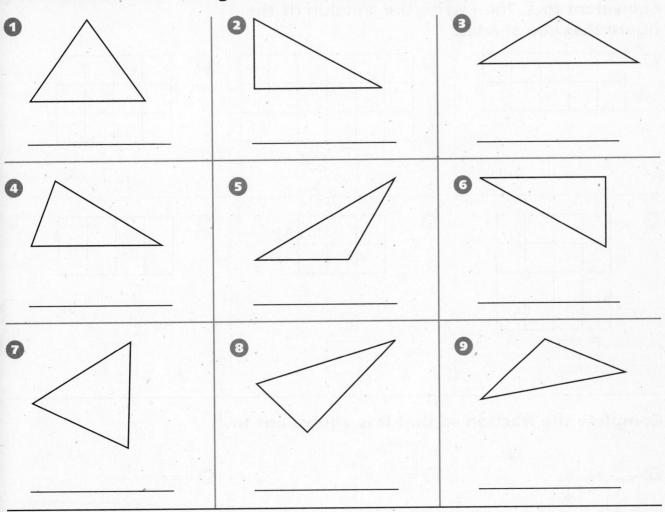

1. 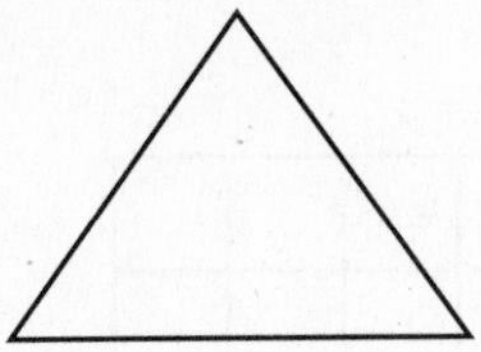
____

2. 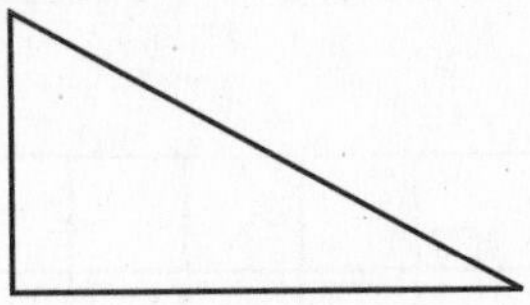
____

3. 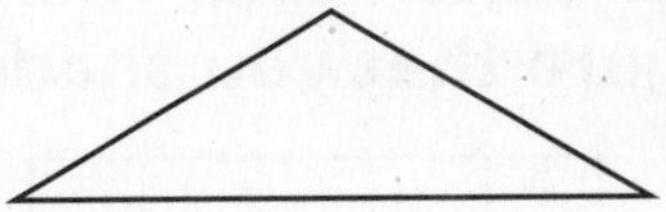
____

4. 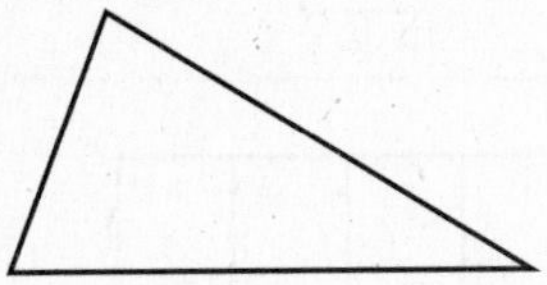
____

5. 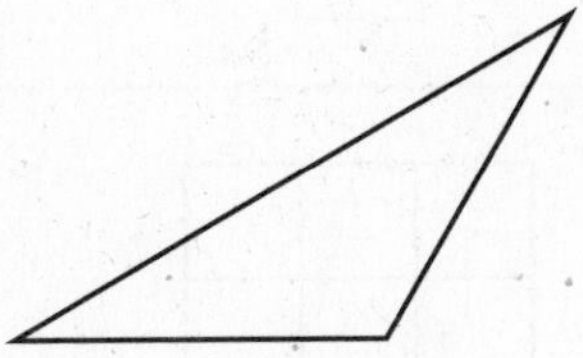
____

6. 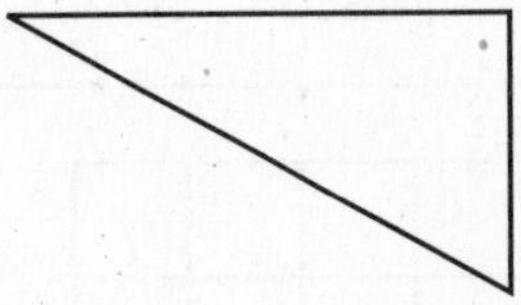
____

7. 
____

8. 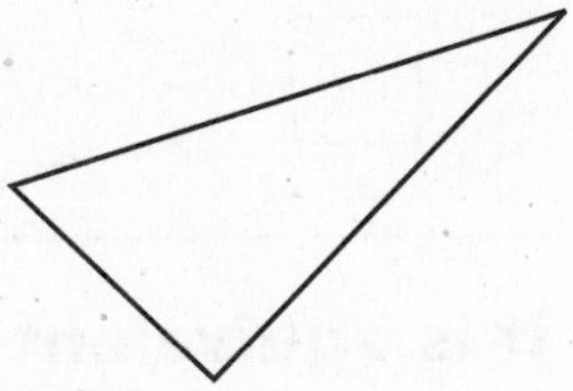
____

9. 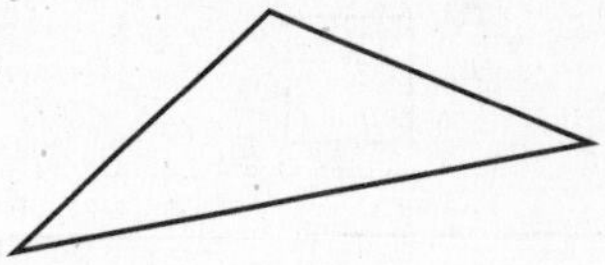
____

Measurement

The thermometer shows the high temperature for a day. Suppose the low temperature for the day was 15° colder. Write the low temperature.

10. °F
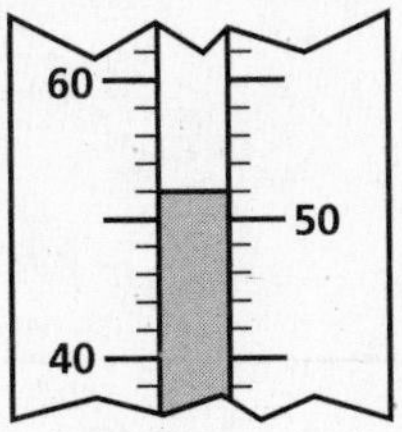

____

11. °F
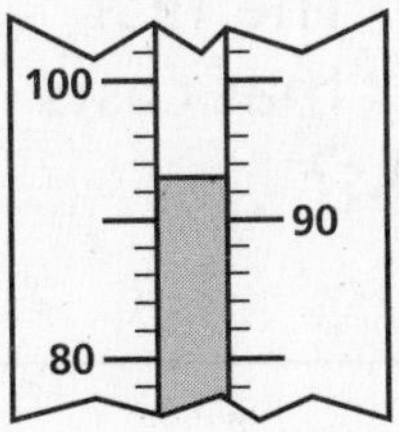

____

12. °F
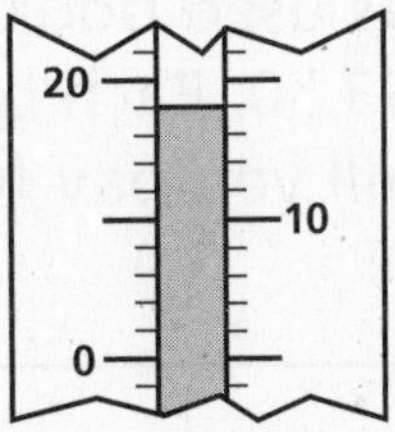

____

13. °F
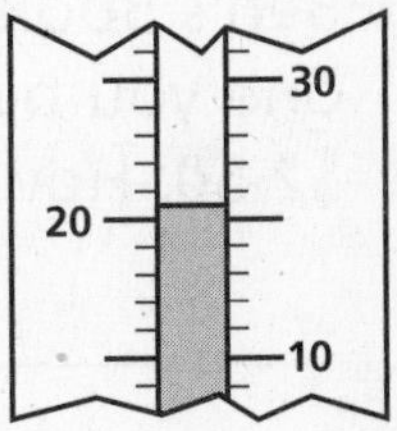

____

Name ______________________ Date ____________

Number and Operations

Shade the figure to show a fraction that is equivalent to $\frac{1}{2}$. Then write the fraction of the figure that you shaded.

1. 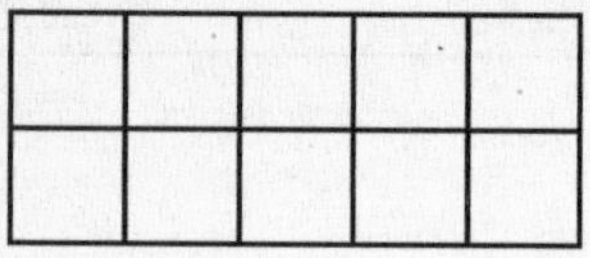
☐

2. 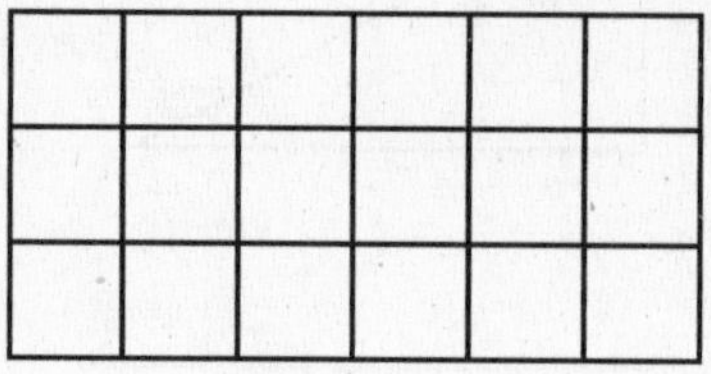
☐

3. 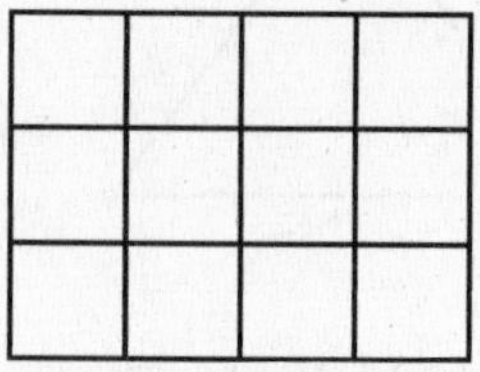
☐

4. 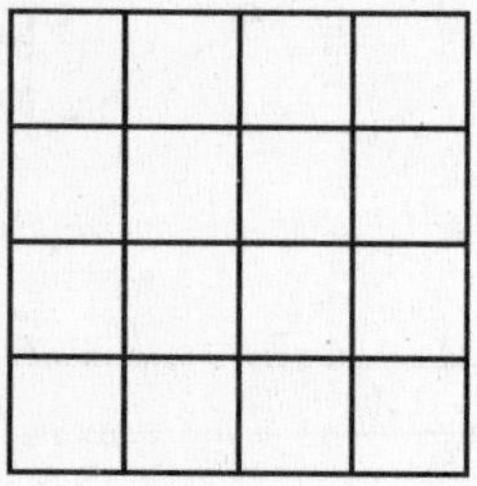
☐

5. 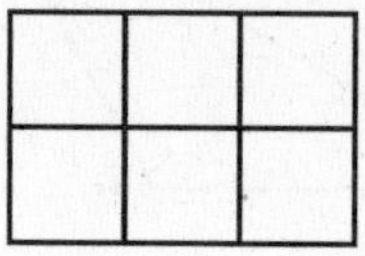
☐

6. 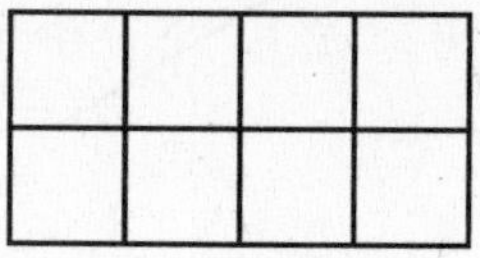
☐

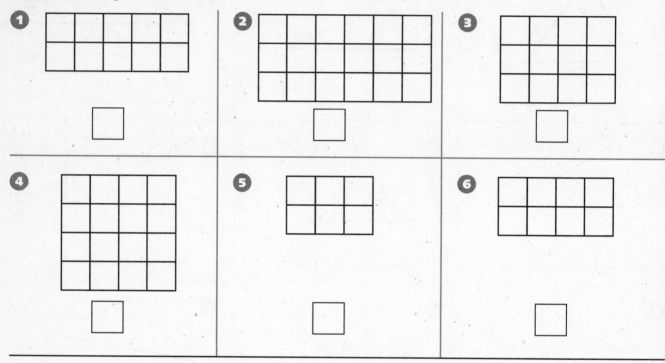

Complete the fraction so that it is equivalent to $\frac{1}{2}$.

7. $\frac{7}{\square} = \frac{1}{2}$

8. $\frac{\square}{20} = \frac{1}{2}$

9. $\frac{\square}{30} = \frac{1}{2}$

Problem Solving

Solve the problem. Explain your answer.

10. Ben's Book Store has used books on sale. The first one you buy costs $3.50. Each book after that costs $2.50. How much will you pay for 8 books?

____

____

Name ______________________________ Date ______________

Spiral Review
Lesson 7

Algebra

Complete each multiplication table.

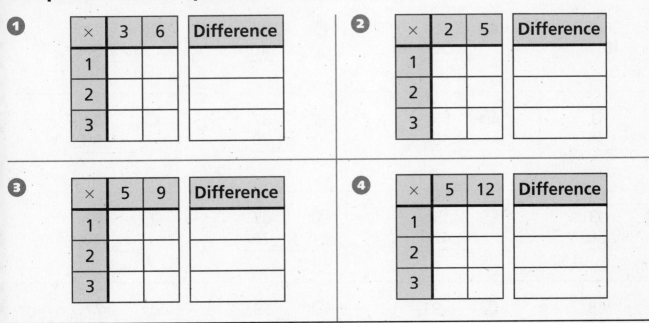

1.

×	3	6	Difference
1			
2			
3			

2.

×	2	5	Difference
1			
2			
3			

3.

×	5	9	Difference
1			
2			
3			

4.

×	5	12	Difference
1			
2			
3			

Geometry

The two figures have the same area. Are they congruent? Write *yes* or *no*. Then find the area of each figure.

5. 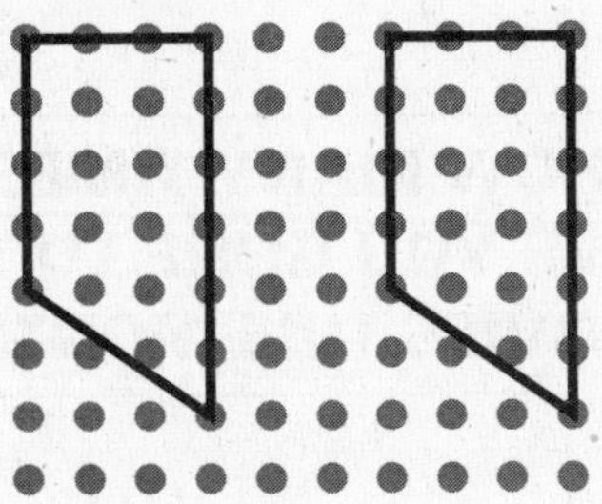

Congruent ______

Area = ☐ square units

6. 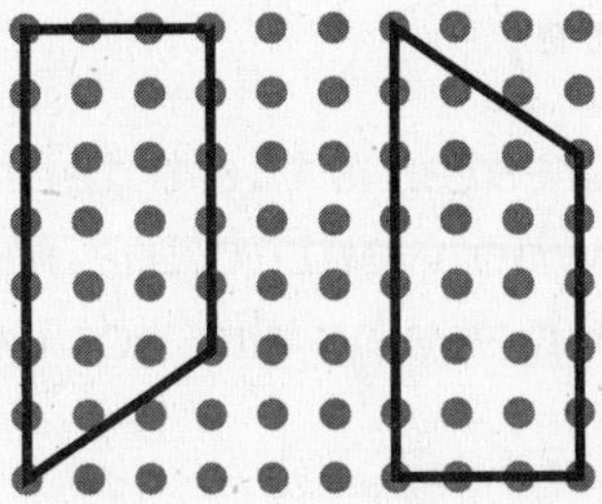

Congruent ______

Area = ☐ square units

Name ______________________ Date ____________

Spiral Review
Lesson 8

Number and Operations

Find the product.

1. 26×10	2. 51×20	3. 78×40	4. 17×60
5. 41×30	6. 55×10	7. 87×70	8. 82×90
9. 93×50	10. 15×40	11. 67×70	12. 62×30
13. 48×90	14. 91×40	15. 59×60	16. 77×80

Data Analysis and Probability

For 17–19, use the bar graph. It shows the results of a class survey.

17. How much greater is the total number of students who went to the movies than the number who did not go at all?

____

18. How many more students went to the movies once than went three or more times?

____

19. There are 27 students in the class. How many of them did NOT take part in the survey?

____

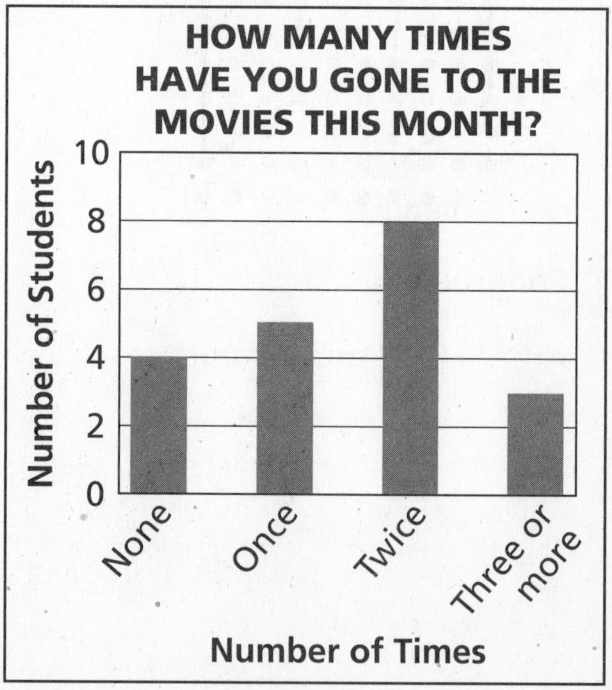

Name ______________________ Date ____________

Measurement

Measure the line segment to the nearest quarter inch.

1 ______________________________ [ ]

2 ____________________________________ [ ]

3 _________________ [ ]

4 ______________________ [ ]

5 ___________________________________ [ ]

6 _________________________________ [ ]

7 ___________________ [ ]

8 ______________________________ [ ]

Problem Solving

Solve the problem. Explain your answer.

9 Vicki weighs her dog Buster on her home scale. Then she weighs herself. When she stands on the scale with her dog, it reads 127 pounds. Vicki weighs 53 pounds more than her dog. How much do they each weigh?

____

____

____

____

____

Name ______________________________ Date ______________

Algebra

Write the rule for the table. Then write the missing numbers.

1

Input	Output
4	12
7	21
1	3
6	
10	

____

2

Input	Output
3	9
5	11
9	15
2	
11	

____

3

Input	Output
13	7
11	5
7	1
9	
12	

____

4

Input	Output
20	10
12	6
14	7
16	
2	

____

Geometry

Write the letters of the figures that are examples of the quadrilateral named.

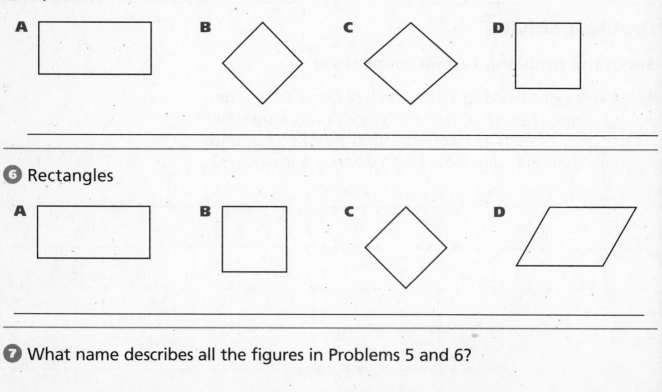

5 Squares

A 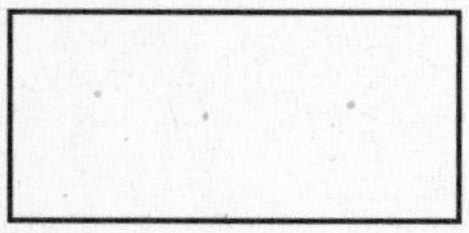

B 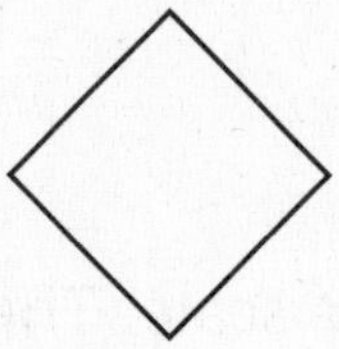

C 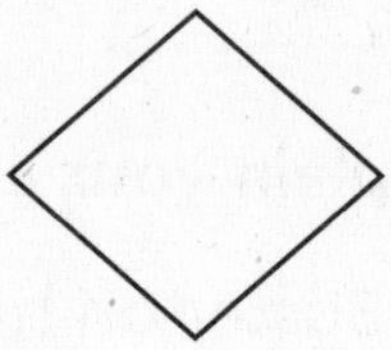

D 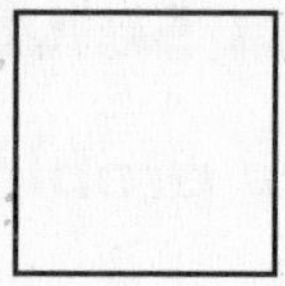

____

6 Rectangles

A 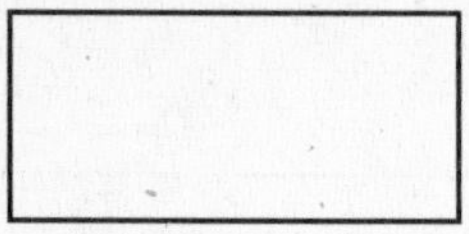

B 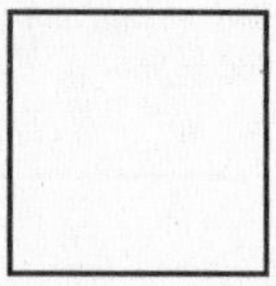

C 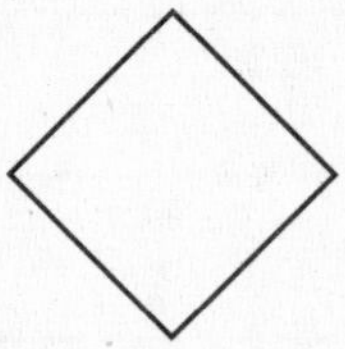

D 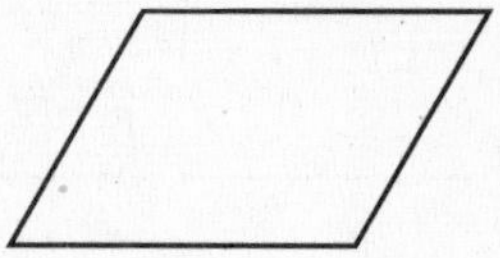

____

7 What name describes all the figures in Problems 5 and 6?

____

Name ______________________ Date ____________

Spiral Review
Lesson 1

Geometry

For 1–4, use the figures. Write the letters of the rectangles that have the same perimeter.

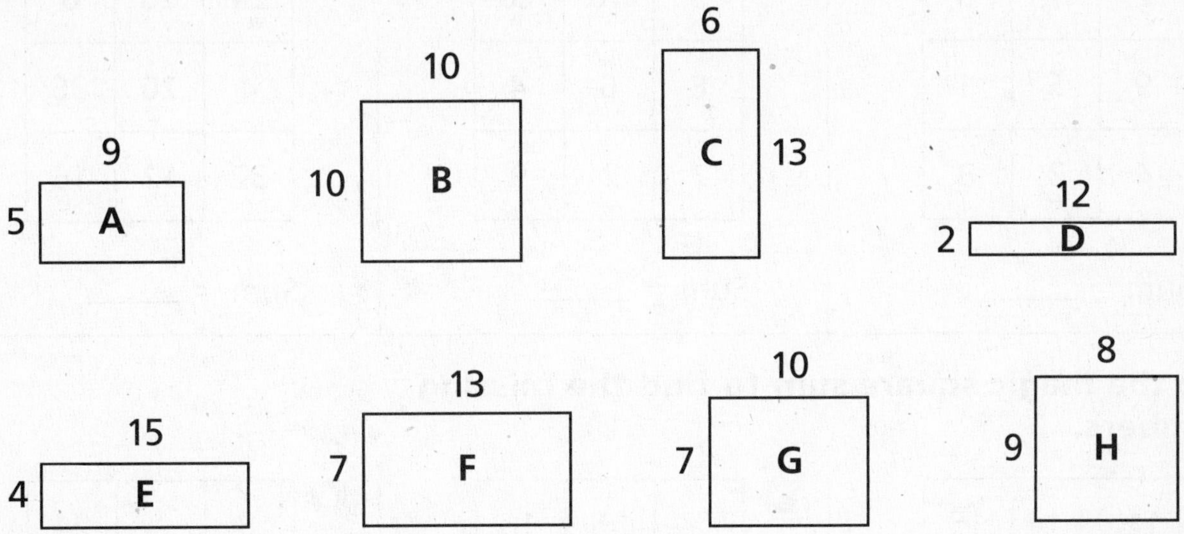

1. ______ and ______
2. ______ and ______
3. ______ and ______
4. ______ and ______

Problem Solving

Solve the problem. Explain your answer.

5. Josh swims 5 days each week. During the first week, he swam 2 laps of the pool each day. During the second week, he swam 4 laps each day. During the third week, he swam 6 laps each day. If he continued this pattern, what is the total number of laps he swam during the fifth week?

____

____

____

Name ____________________ Date __________

Number and Operations

Find the sum of each magic square.

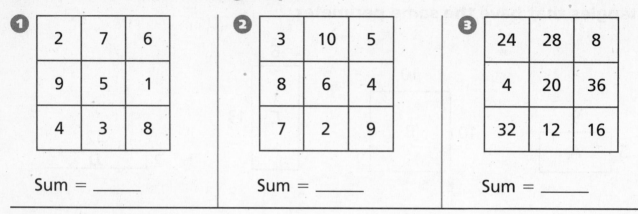

1

2	7	6
9	5	1
4	3	8

Sum = ______

2

3	10	5
8	6	4
7	2	9

Sum = ______

3

24	28	8
4	20	36
32	12	16

Sum = ______

Use the magic square sum to find the missing numbers.

4

11	1	15
13		5
3	17	

5

	56	16
8	40	
64	24	32

6

8		24
36	20	
16	12	32

Data Analysis and Probability

For 7–8, use the bar graph.

7 The students saw 41 birds. How many birds were NOT penguins?

____

8 The students saw 33 cats in all. How many times greater was the number of cats that were not tigers than the number that were tigers?

____

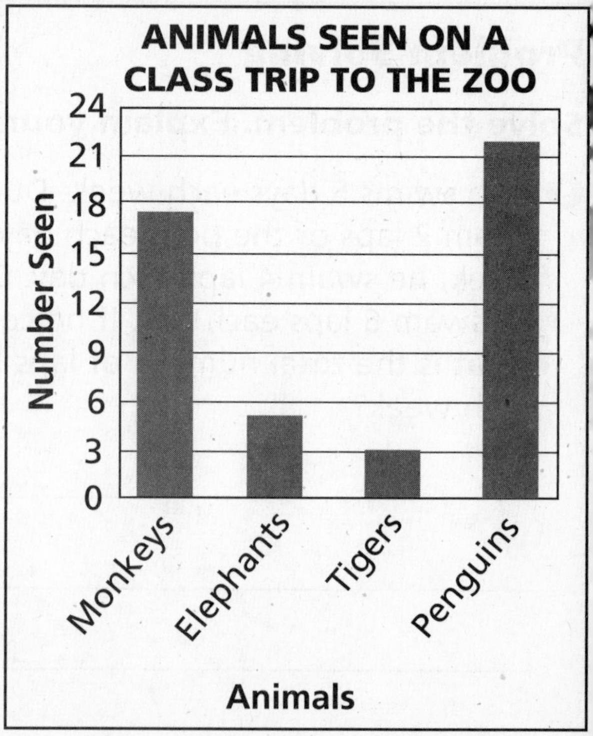

Name ______________________ Date ______________

Spiral Review
Lesson 3

Algebra

Write the number or numbers that make the sentence true.

1. 8 × ______ = 32 32 ÷ 4 = 8	2. 6 × ______ = 30 30 ÷ 6 = 5	3. ______ × 9 = 27 27 ÷ 9 = ______
4. 4 × ______ = 24 24 ÷ ______ = 6	5. 8 × ______ = 40 40 ÷ ______ = 5	6. 35 ÷ ______ = 5 5 × ______ = 35
7. 56 ÷ 7 = ______ ______ × 7 = 56	8. 72 ÷ 9 = ______ 9 × ______ = 72	9. 9 × 9 = 81 81 ÷ ______ = 9
10. 10 × ______ = 70 70 ÷ ______ = 7	11. 63 ÷ 9 = ______ ______ × 9 = 63	12. 6 × ______ = 54 54 ÷ 6 = ______

Problem Solving

Solve the problem. Explain your answer.

13. A snail fell into a hole that was 7 feet deep. Each day, it climbed 3 feet up the side, but each night it slid back 1 foot. How many days did it take the snail to reach the top of the hole?

____

____

____

____

____

____

Name ______________________ Date ______________

Spiral Review
Lesson 4

Geometry

Write *perpendicular, parallel,* or *neither* to describe the pair of lines.

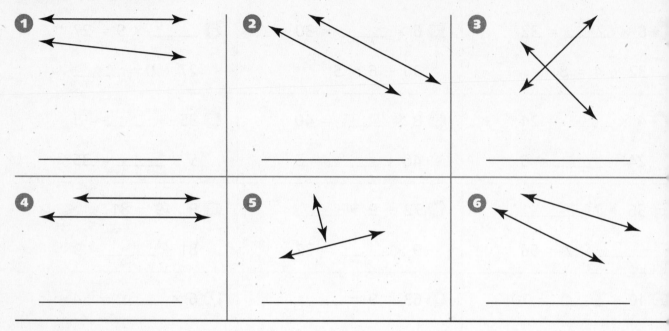

1. 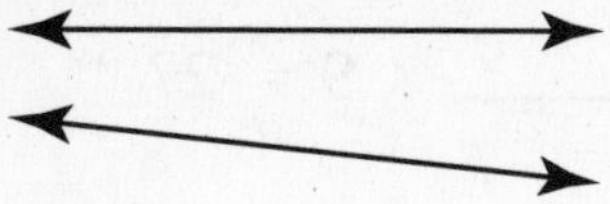
____

2. 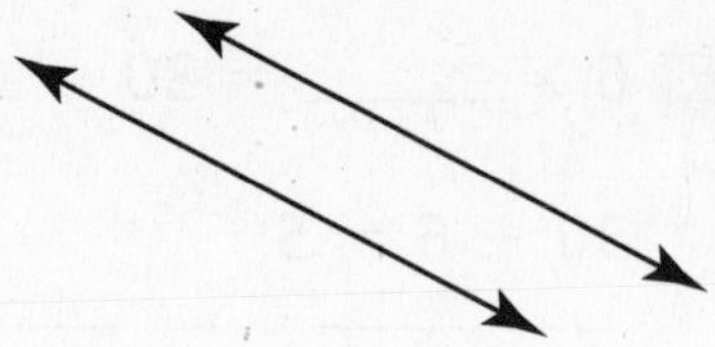
____

3. 
____

4. 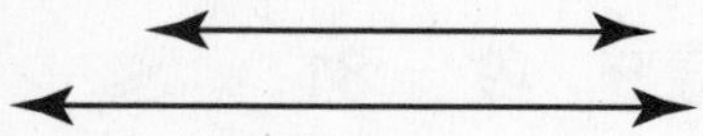
____

5. 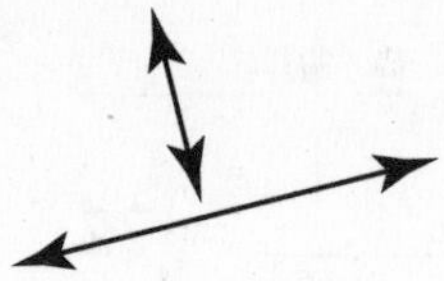
____

6. 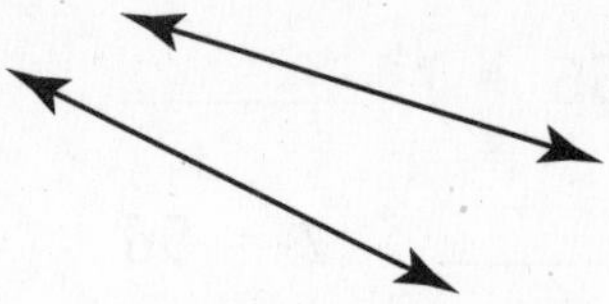
____

Measurement

Find the sum or difference.

7. $0.93 + $0.87

8. $2.07 − $1.28

9. $0.11 + $0.75

10. $1.00 − $0.66

11. $0.89 + $0.45

12. $1.00 − $0.10

13. $0.33 + $0.55

14. $0.98 − $0.69

15. $2.00 − $1.76

16. $10.00 − $1.76

17. $10.00 − $3.76

Name ______________________ Date ______________

Spiral Review
Lesson 5

Number and Operations

Find the number of squares in each of the two sections. Then find the total in the array.

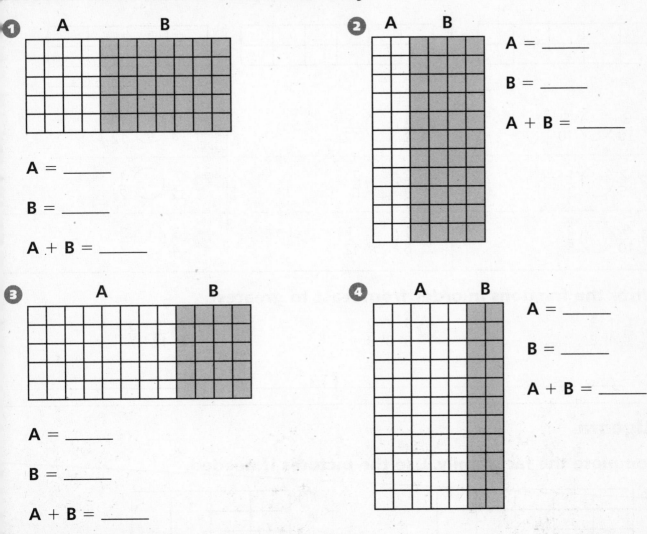

1

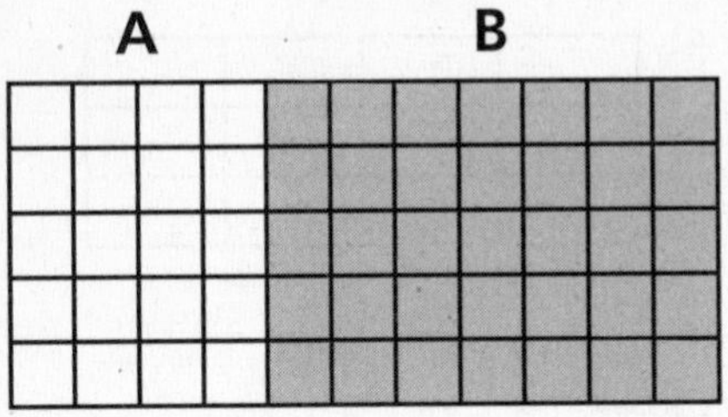

A = ______

B = ______

A + B = ______

2

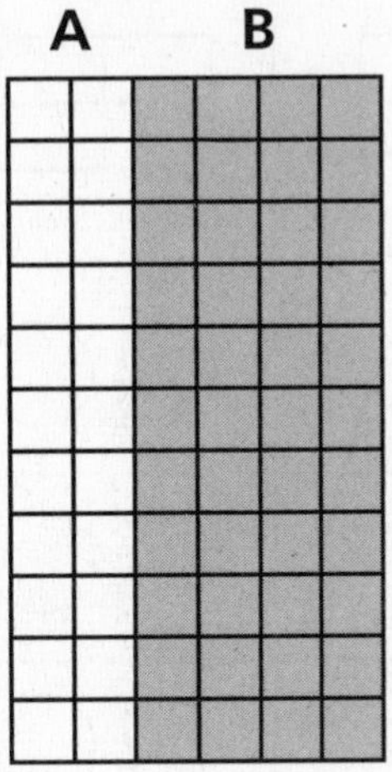

A = ______

B = ______

A + B = ______

3

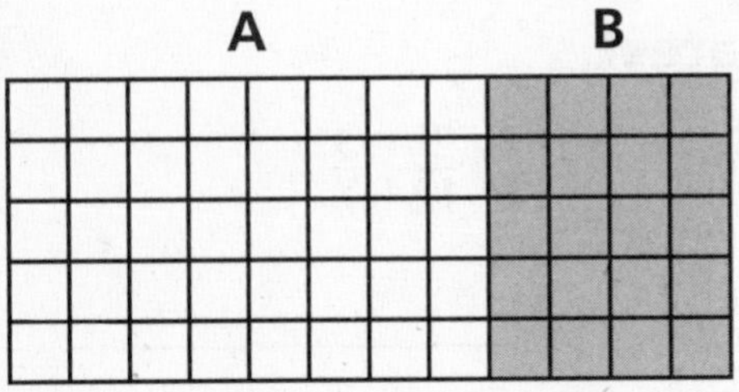

A = ______

B = ______

A + B = ______

4

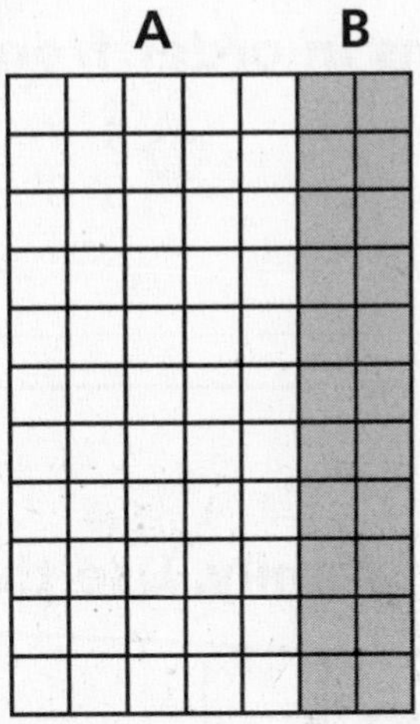

A = ______

B = ______

A + B = ______

Problem Solving

Solve the problem. Explain your answer.

5 A school cafeteria has square tables. Only 1 student can sit on a side. If 2 tables are put together end-to-end, 6 students can sit at the larger table. How many students can sit at a table made by putting 20 tables end-to-end?

____

____

Name ____________________ Date ____________

Spiral Review
Lesson 6

Number and Operations

Write < or > to compare the fractions. Use the diagrams at the top of each column to help you.

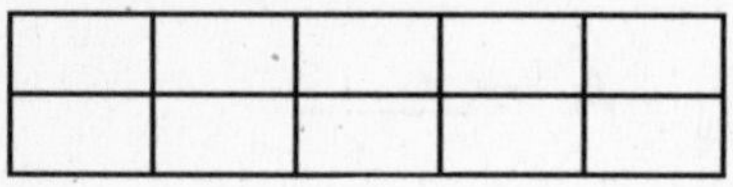

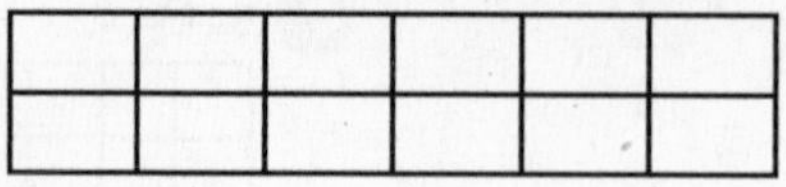

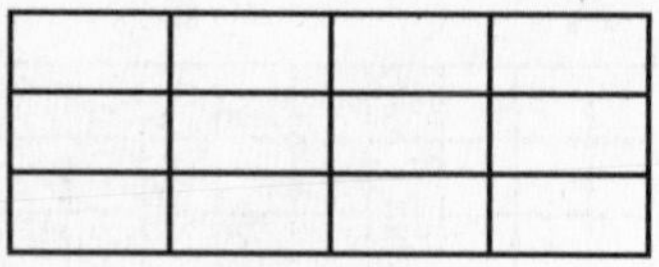

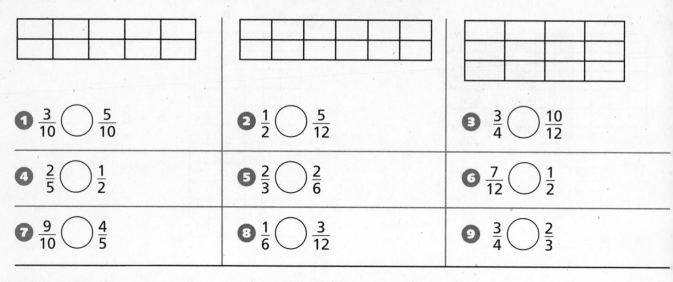

1. $\frac{3}{10}$ ◯ $\frac{5}{10}$
2. $\frac{1}{2}$ ◯ $\frac{5}{12}$
3. $\frac{3}{4}$ ◯ $\frac{10}{12}$
4. $\frac{2}{5}$ ◯ $\frac{1}{2}$
5. $\frac{2}{3}$ ◯ $\frac{2}{6}$
6. $\frac{7}{12}$ ◯ $\frac{1}{2}$
7. $\frac{9}{10}$ ◯ $\frac{4}{5}$
8. $\frac{1}{6}$ ◯ $\frac{3}{12}$
9. $\frac{3}{4}$ ◯ $\frac{2}{3}$

Write the fractions in order from least to greatest.

10. $\frac{1}{3}, \frac{1}{4}, \frac{3}{8}$ ____________________
11. $\frac{5}{6}, \frac{7}{8}, \frac{2}{3}$ ____________________
12. $\frac{2}{5}, \frac{9}{12}, \frac{3}{7}$ ____________________

Algebra

Complete the fact family. Use the pictures if needed.

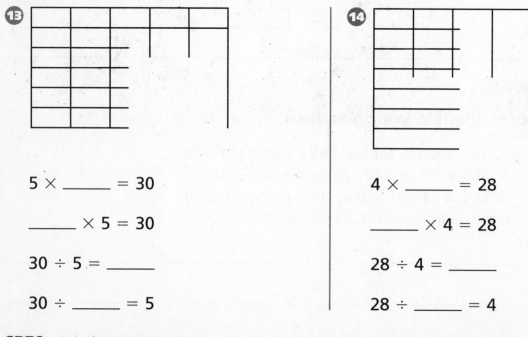

13.

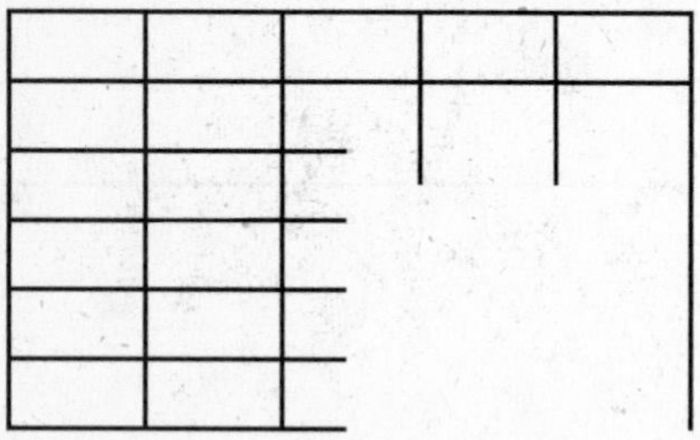

5 × ______ = 30

______ × 5 = 30

30 ÷ 5 = ______

30 ÷ ______ = 5

14.

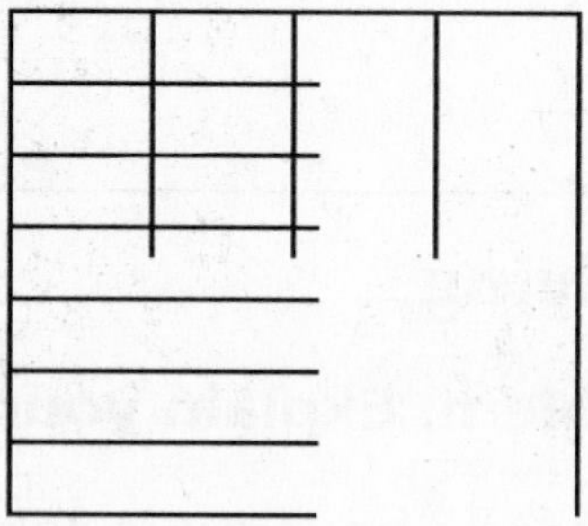

4 × ______ = 28

______ × 4 = 28

28 ÷ 4 = ______

28 ÷ ______ = 4

Name ______________________ Date ____________

Spiral Review
Lesson 7

Geometry

Which angle is larger?

1. 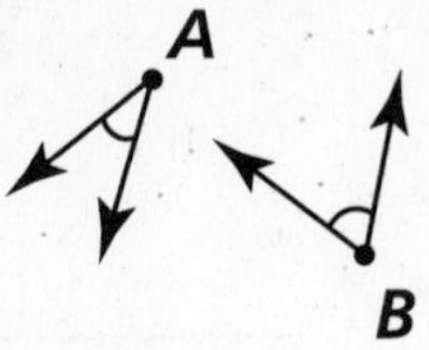

______

2. 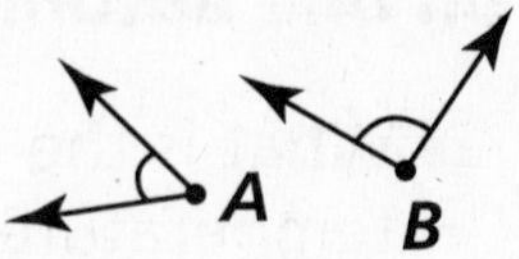

______

3. 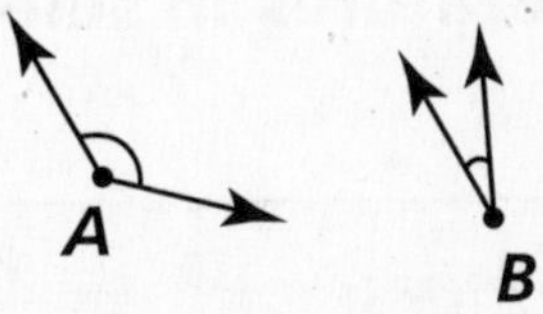

______

Write the angles in order from smallest to largest.

4. 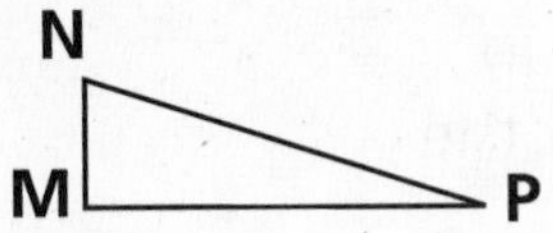

____

5. 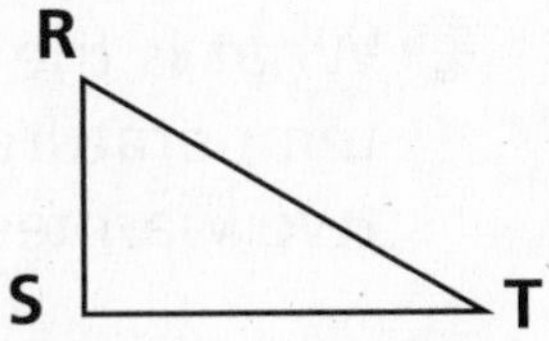

____

6. 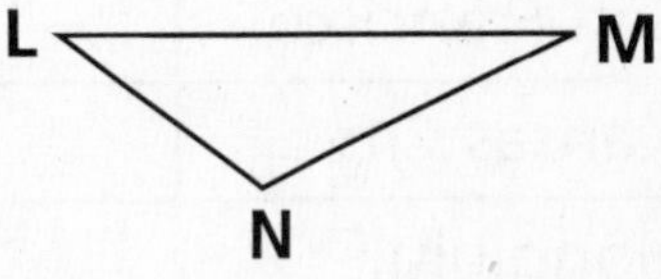

____

Data Analysis and Probability

For 7–8, write *impossible* or *possible*.

7. A new student will come into your class before the end of the year. ______________

8. Next week, there will be no Friday. ______________

Choose the event that is the more likely of the two.

9. getting an even number or getting a number less than 3 when you roll a 1–6 number cube

____

10. getting an even number or getting a number greater than 3 when you draw one of 8 cards marked 1–8

____

Name ______________________ Date __________

Measurement

For 1–5, use the table, which shows the high temperatures in selected cities on one autumn day.

City	High Temperature
New York City	54°F
Dallas	71°F
Anchorage	19°F
San Francisco	47°F
Kansas City	67°F
Honolulu	81°F

1. What is the difference in temperatures between the warmest and coolest cities? __________

2. What is the difference in temperatures between San Francisco and New York City? __________

3. What is the difference in temperatures between the two warmest cities? __________

4. What is the difference in temperatures between the two coolest cities? __________

5. The day after these temperatures were recorded, the temperature in Dallas was 87°F. How many degrees warmer was Dallas than it had been the day before? __________

Reasoning and Proof

Complete the magic square. Then write the sum.

6.

7	12	
	10	6
9		13

Sum = ______

7.

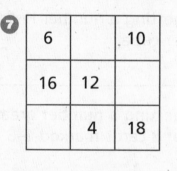

6		10
16	12	
	4	18

Sum = ______

8.

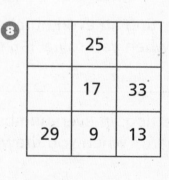

	25	
	17	33
29	9	13

Sum = ______

Name ______________________ Date ______________

Spiral Review
Lesson 9

Geometry

**Decide whether the line is a line of symmetry.
Write *yes* or *no*.**

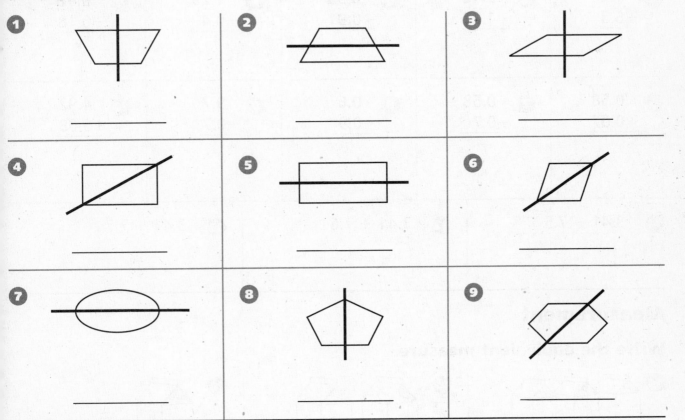

1. 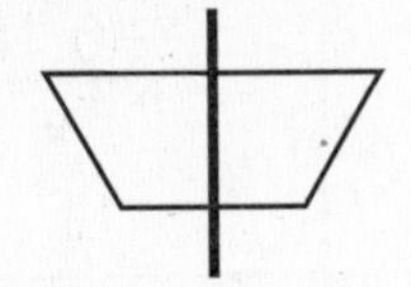

2. 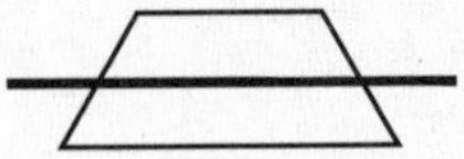

3. 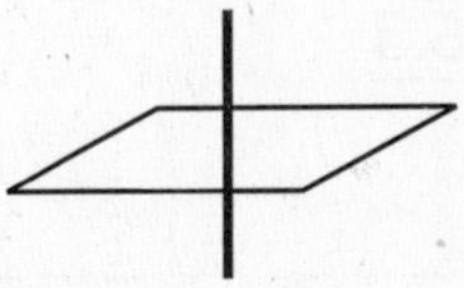

4. 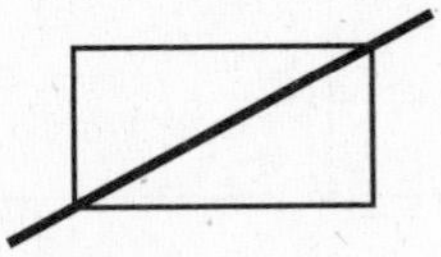

5. 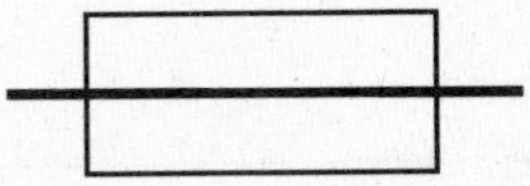

6. 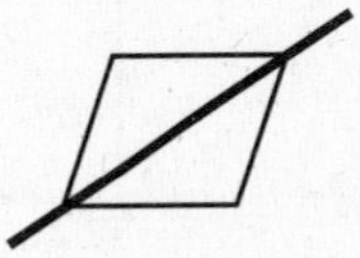

7. 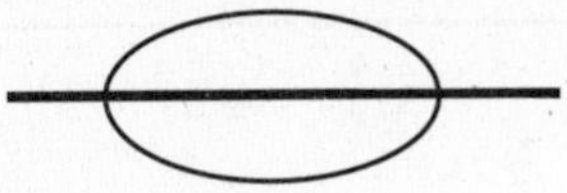

8. 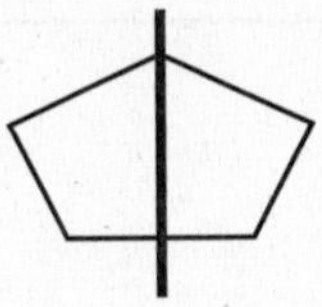

9. 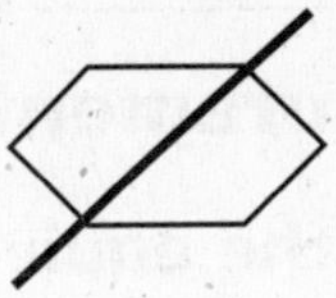

Problem Solving

Solve the problem. Explain your answer.

10. Together, John and Andrea make 92 cards to give to friends. John makes 16 more cards than Andrea. How many cards do they each make?

11. Kyle has $2.55 in his pocket. If he has only quarters and nickels and has 3 more quarters than nickels, how many of each coin does he have?

Name ______________________ Date ______________

Spiral Review
Lesson 10

Number and Operations

Find the sum.

1. $\begin{array}{r} 1.4 \\ +6.3 \\ \hline \end{array}$

2. $\begin{array}{r} 2.12 \\ +1.27 \\ \hline \end{array}$

3. $\begin{array}{r} 0.35 \\ +0.91 \\ \hline \end{array}$

4. $\begin{array}{r} 1.29 \\ +0.4 \\ \hline \end{array}$

5. $\begin{array}{r} 0.92 \\ +0.18 \\ \hline \end{array}$

6. $\begin{array}{r} 0.58 \\ +0.07 \\ \hline \end{array}$

7. $\begin{array}{r} 0.58 \\ +0.7 \\ \hline \end{array}$

8. $\begin{array}{r} 0.6 \\ +0.9 \\ \hline \end{array}$

9. $\begin{array}{r} 9.7 \\ +0.7 \\ \hline \end{array}$

10. $\begin{array}{r} 4.92 \\ +5.08 \\ \hline \end{array}$

11. 3.41 + 7.5

12. 3.41 + 7.6

13. 3.41 + 7.7

Measurement

Write the equivalent measure.

14. 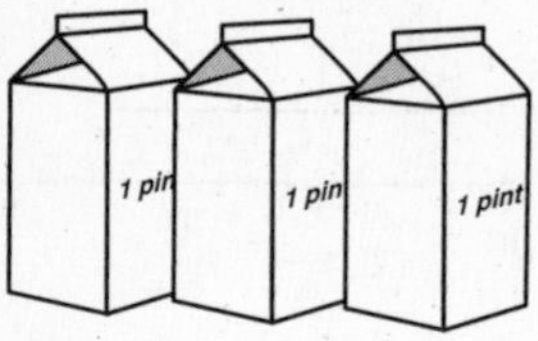

_____ cups

15. 

_____ pints

16. 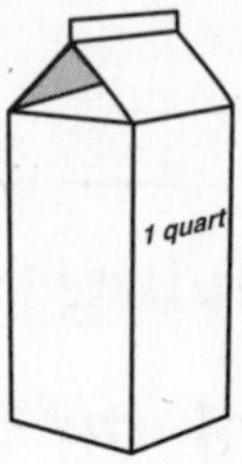

_____ cups

17. 

_____ pints

18. 

_____ quarts

19. 

_____ cups

Name ______________________ Date ______________

Number and Operations

Use the number line. Write the letter that matches the number.

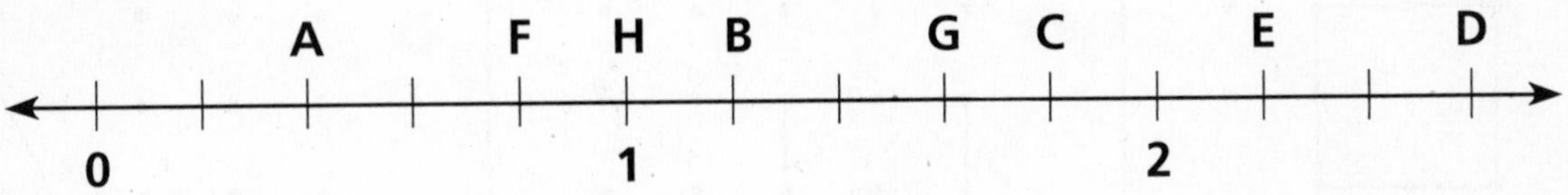

1. 2.2 ______
2. 0.4 ______
3. 1.8 ______
4. 1.0 ______
5. 0.8 ______
6. 1.2 ______
7. 2.6 ______
8. 1.6 ______

Problem Solving

Solve the problem. Explain your answer.

9. Katrina is standing on the middle step of a ladder. She climbs up one step and then down 3 steps so that there are 2 steps below her. How many steps does the ladder have?

____

____

____

10. Eliza did some chores after school and earned $4 per hour. Then she got $20 for a birthday present and had $32 in all. For how many hours did she do chores?

____

____

____

Name ______________________ Date ____________

Geometry

Find the area of the figure. The area of the smallest square on the dot grid is 1 square unit.

1. 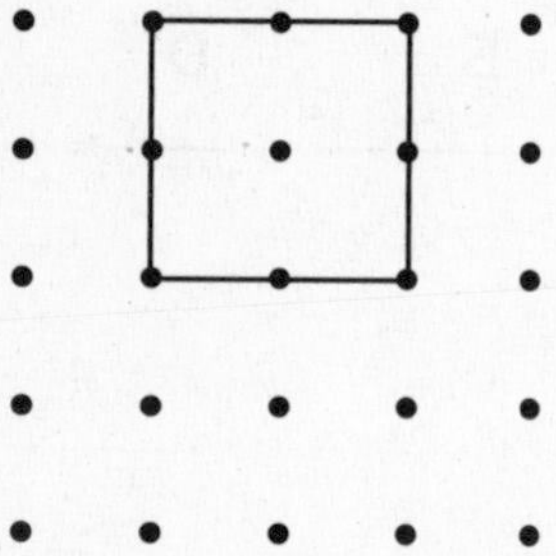
____

2. 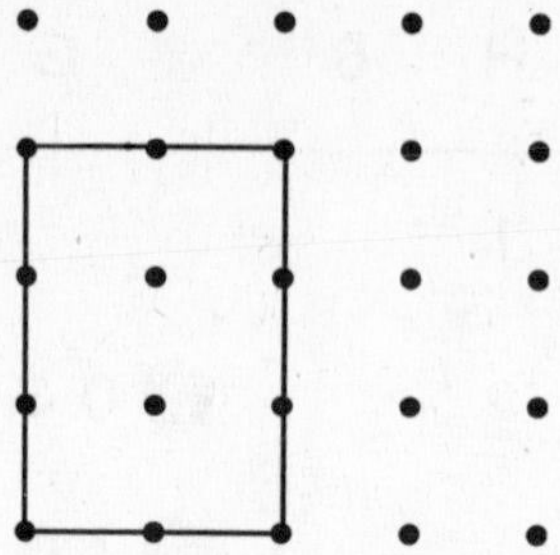
____

3. 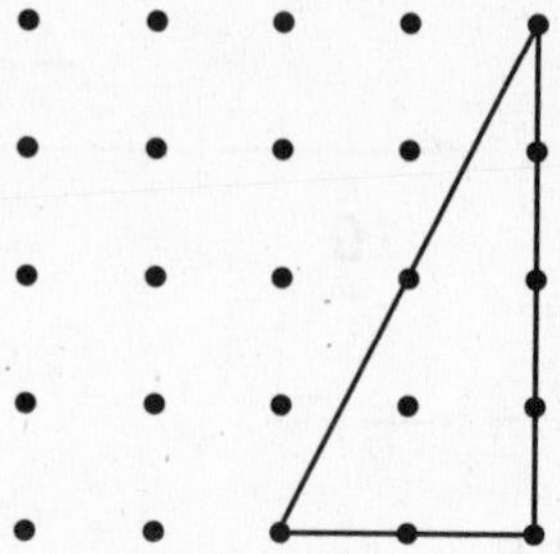
____

4. 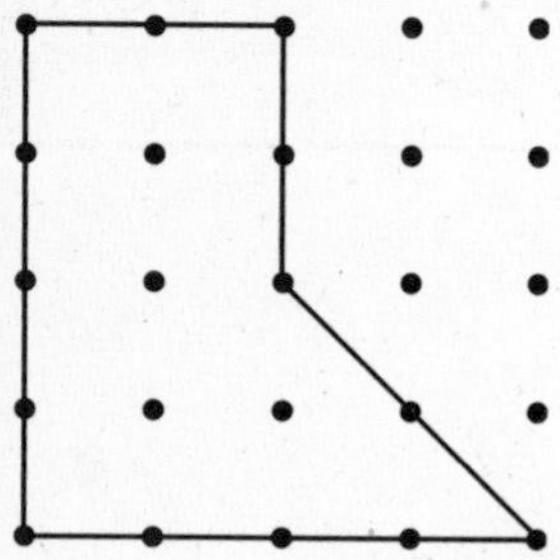
____

5. 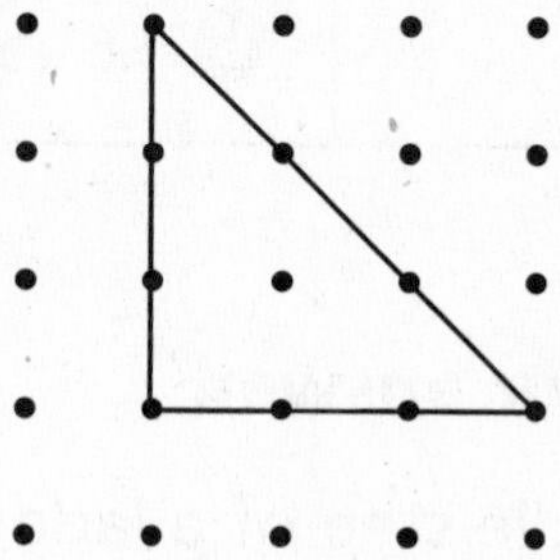
____

6. 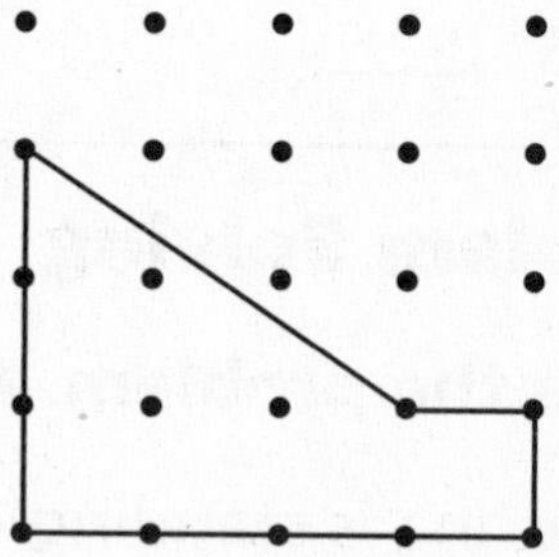
____

Algebra

Complete the last two rows of the table. Then write a rule for the table.

7.

Week	Saved
1	$1.00
2	$3.00
3	$5.00
4	$7.00
5	
6	

____

8.

Books	Pens
3	6
4	8
5	10
6	12
7	
8	

____

9.

Wheels	Tricycles
27	9
24	8
21	7
18	6
15	
12	

____

Name ______________________ Date ____________

Spiral Review
Lesson 3

Measurement

Circle the larger measurement.

1 17 inches or $1\frac{1}{2}$ feet	2 1 yard or 2 feet 15 inches
3 2 yards or 5 feet	4 31 inches or 2 feet 6 inches
5 51 inches or $2\frac{1}{2}$ yards	6 $1\frac{1}{4}$ feet or 19 inches

Reasoning and Proof

For 7–11, use the graph.

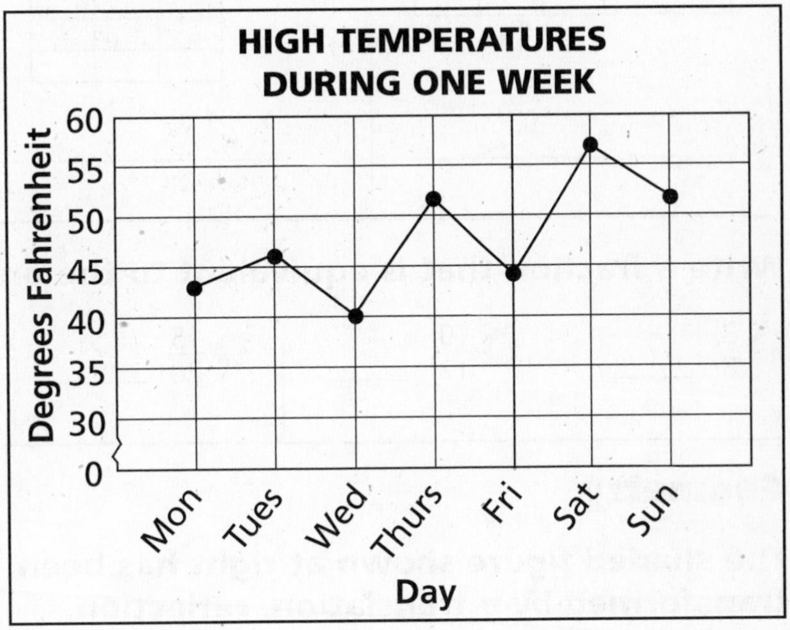

7 Which was the warmest day of the week?

____

8 On how many days was the high temperature above 50°F?

____

9 At which two days would you look to find the difference between the warmest high temperature and the coolest?

____

10 Estimate the difference between the warmest high temperature and the coolest.

____

11 Describe the changes in the high temperatures for the week.

____

____

Name ______________________ Date ______________

Number and Operations

Write a pair of equivalent fractions for the shaded part of the figure.

1. 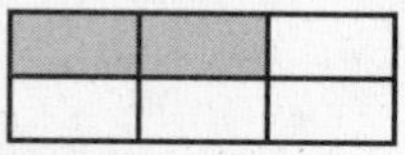

____

2. 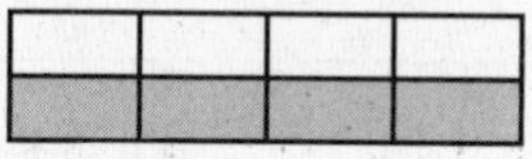

____

3. 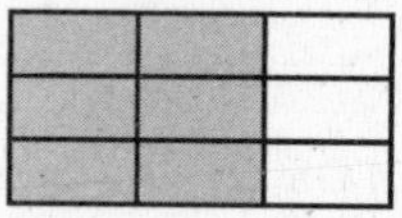

____

4. 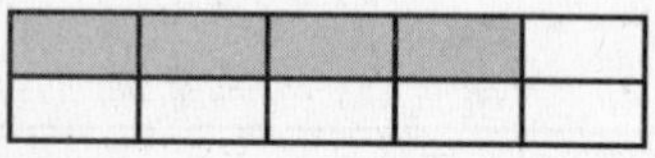

____

5. 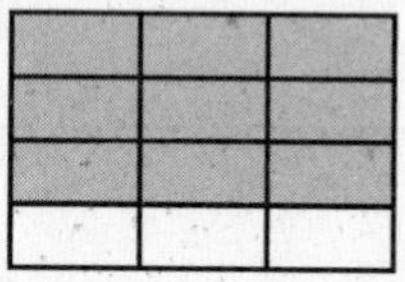

____

6. 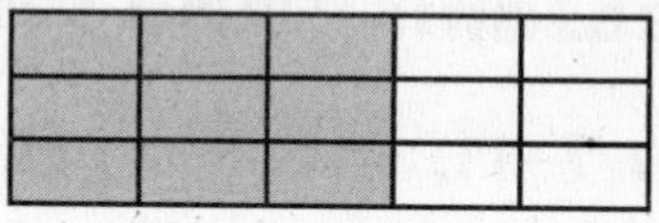

____

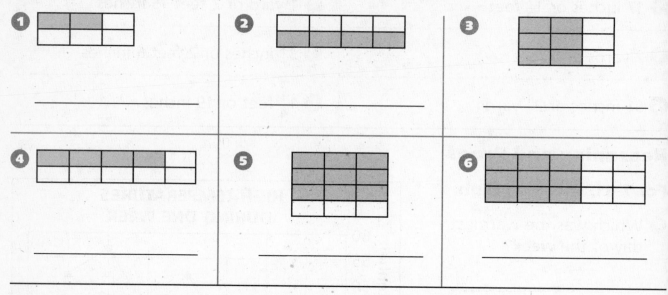

Write a fraction that is equivalent to the one given.

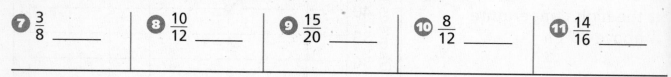

7. $\frac{3}{8}$ ______

8. $\frac{10}{12}$ ______

9. $\frac{15}{20}$ ______

10. $\frac{8}{12}$ ______

11. $\frac{14}{16}$ ______

Geometry

The shaded figure shown at right has been transformed by a translation, reflection, or rotation.

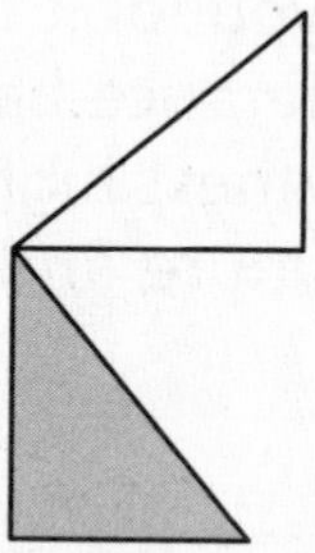

12. Which transformation, if any, changes the size or shape of the original figure?

____

13. How could you show that the two figures are congruent?

____

____

____

Name ______________________ Date ____________

Spiral Review
Lesson 5

Number and Operations

Find the sum.

1 381 + 219	2 745 + 89	3 422 + 199	4 611 + 928
5 86 + 85 + 21	6 108 + 98 + 85	7 47 + 76 + 754	8 96 + 175 + 36

Find the difference.

9 351 − 194	10 520 − 359	11 792 − 225	12 905 − 689

Find the product.

13 32 × 41	14 63 × 19	15 107 × 96	16 229 × 35

Find the quotient.

17 96 ÷ 8	18 119 ÷ 7	19 504 ÷ 9	20 221 ÷ 17

Problem Solving

Solve the problem. Explain your answer.

21 Andrew has 3 new books to put on his shelf. In how many different orders can he put the books?

Name ______________________ Date ____________

Spiral Review
Lesson 6

Algebra

Look for shortcuts to help you complete the tables.

1.

	5	7	10	11	12
× 2					

	5	7	10	11	12
× 4					

	5	7	10	11	12
× 6					

2.

	3	6	8	13	15
× 3					

	3	6	8	13	15
× 5					

	3	6	8	13	15
× 8					

Measurement

Circle the more appropriate unit to measure.

3. the amount of water in a small swimming pool. quart gallon
4. the amount of ice cream in one serving. cup quart
5. the amount of lemonade in a pitcher. quart cup

Complete each sentence.

6. You need ______ cups to fill a quart container that has 1 cup of water in it.

7. You need ______ pints of ice cream to fill a 1-gallon container.

8. You need ______ cups to fill a 1-quart container that has 1 pint of milk in it.

9. You need ______ quart to fill a gallon jug that has 3 quarts of juice in it.

10. You need ______ cups to fill an empty pint container.

11. You need ______ pints to fill a 1-gallon container that is half full of orange juice.

Name ____________________ Date ____________

Spiral Review
Lesson 7

Number and Operations

Write a multiplication sentence for the array.

1 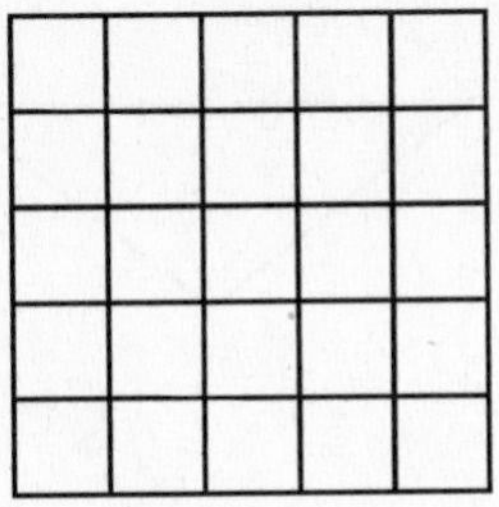

____

2 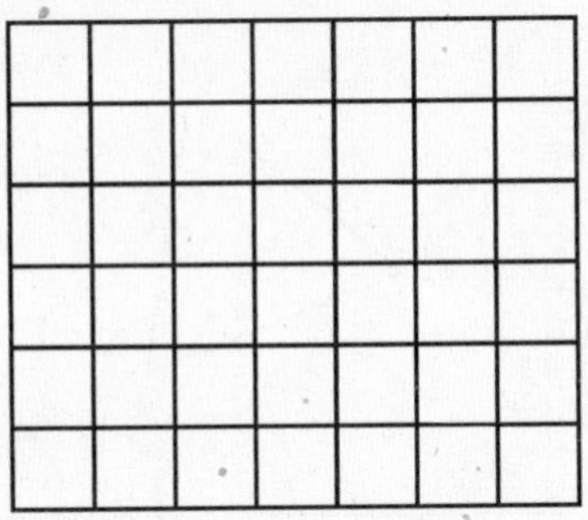

____

3 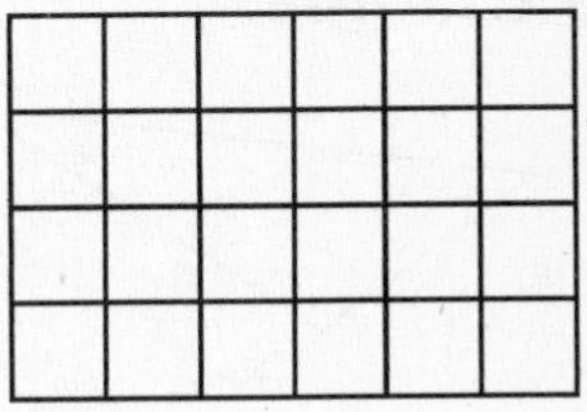

____

4 

____

5 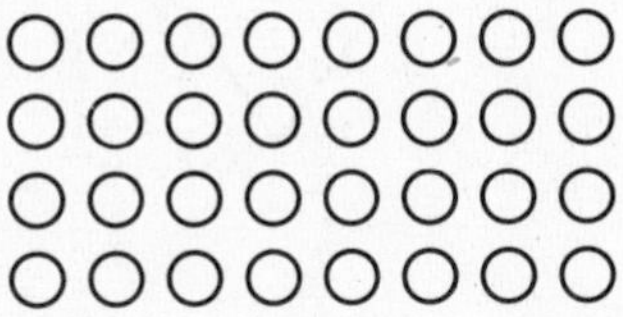

____

6 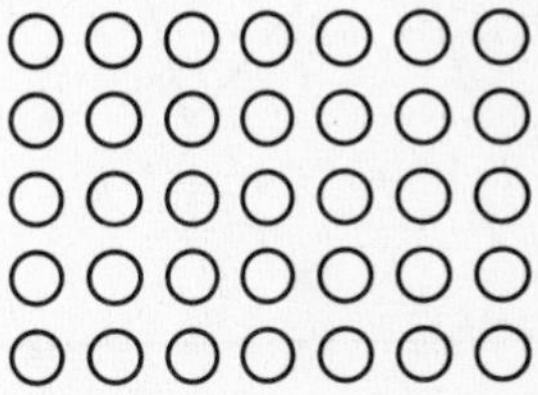

____

Problem Solving

Solve the problem. Explain your answer.

7 A school tennis tournament has 8 players. Each player plays until he or she loses one game and is eliminated. How many games will be needed to find the tournament winner?

____

____

8 Ramon's locker combination is a two-digit number. He can't remember the first digit, but he knows it is either 3, 5, 7, or 9. How many different combinations could he try if the lock shows numbers from 0 to 9?

____

____

Name ______________________ Date ____________

Geometry

Write *scalene, isosceles,* or *equilateral* to describe the triangle.

1. 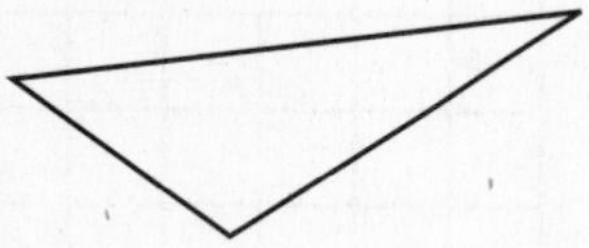
   ____

2. 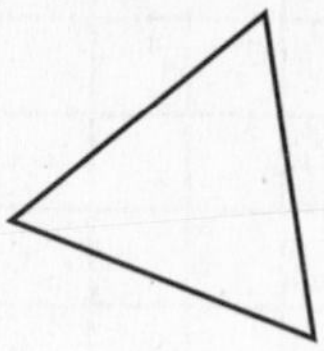
   ____

3. 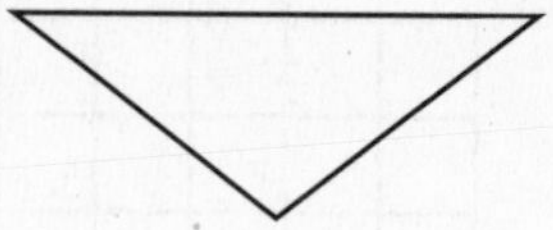
   ____

4. 
   ____

5. 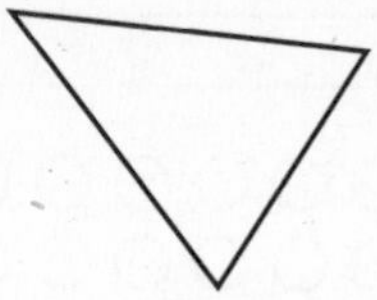
   ____

6. 
   ____

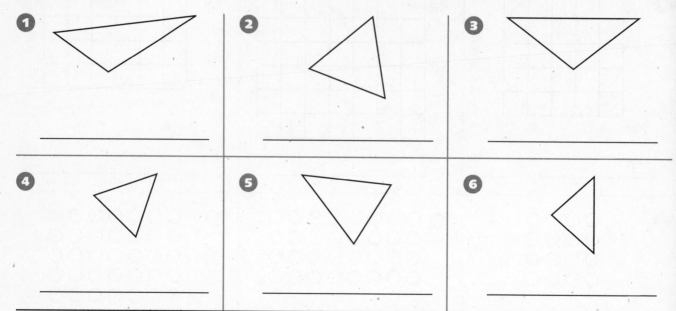

Data Analysis and Probability

A set of cards numbered from 1 to 20 is shuffled and turned upside down. One card is pulled from the deck of cards. Write *impossible, unlikely, likely,* or *certain* for each event.

7. The card will be a number greater than 15. ____________
8. The card will have a number on it greater than 20. ____________
9. The card will have a number on it between 2 and 16. ____________
10. The number on the card will be either even or odd. ____________
11. The number on the card will be a multiple of 5. ____________
12. The number on the card will be a multiple of 21. ____________
13. The number on the card will be your age in years. ____________
14. The number on the card will be either even or a number less than 18. ____________

Name ______________________ Date ____________

Spiral Review
Lesson 1

Number and Operations

Find the difference.

1. 9.4 − 6.7	2. 5.2 − 1.9	3. 1.70 − 0.18	4. 27.2 − 8.6	5. 12.5 − 10.9
6. 4.02 − 2.70	7. 56.33 − 41.14	8. 6.3 − 0.9	9. 26.07 − 22.7	10. 91.82 − 56.71

11. 10.11 − 8.9 = ______
12. 0.31 − 0.22 = ______
13. 15 − 4.2 = ______
14. 1.43 − 0.97 = ______
15. 103.4 − 74.6 = ______
16. 10.2 − 1.8 = ______
17. 20 − 9.98 = ______
18. 122.6 − 99.1 = ______
19. 15.05 − 8.7 = ______
20. 159.1 − 109.1 = ______

Measurement

Write the equivalent measure.

21. 18 inches = ______ feet
22. 1 yard = ______ inches
23. 5 feet = ______ inches
24. 36 inches = ______ feet
25. 48 inches = ______ feet
26. $1\frac{1}{4}$ feet = ______ inches
27. $3\frac{1}{2}$ yards = ______ inches
28. $1\frac{1}{2}$ yards = ______ feet
29. 42 inches = ______ yards
30. 60 inches = ______ yards
31. $1\frac{1}{2}$ yards = ______ inches
32. 24 inches = ______ yard
33. 20 inches = ______ foot ______ inches
34. 72 inches = ______ yards

Name ______________________ Date ______________

Spiral Review
Lesson 2

Geometry

Find the area of the figure. The area of the smallest square is 1 square centimeter.

1. 

Area = ______ cm^2

2.  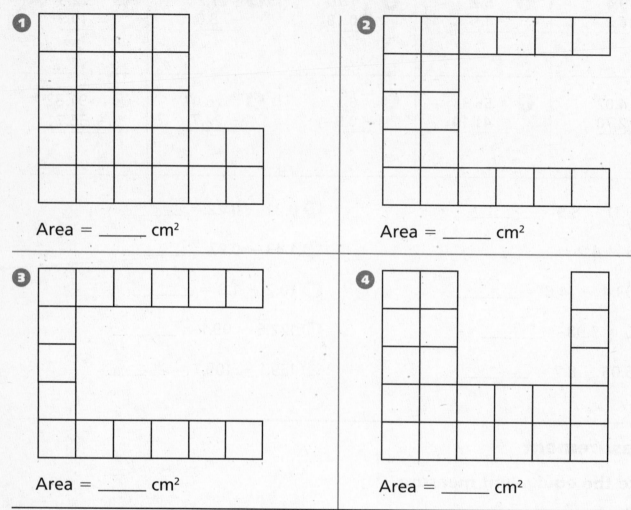

Area = ______ cm^2

3. 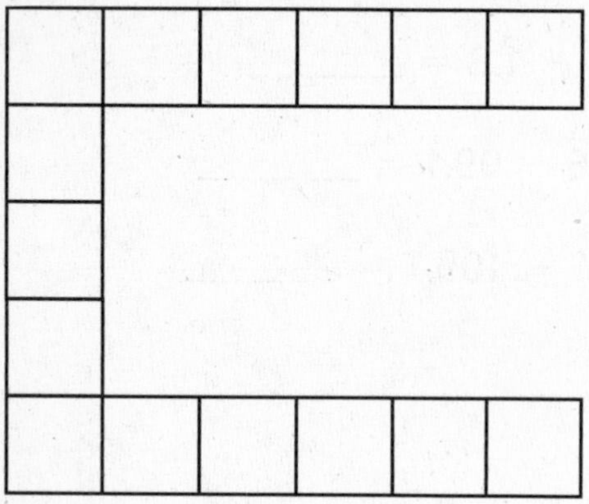

Area = ______ cm^2

4. 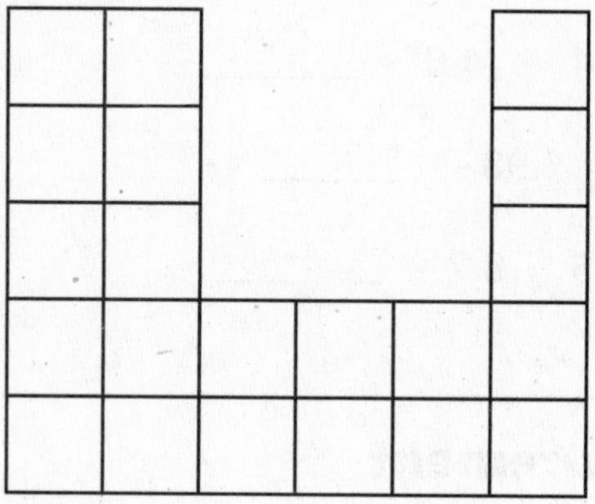

Area = ______ cm^2

Data Analysis and Probability

You toss a 1–6 number cube. Write the more likely event. If the events are equally likely, write *equally likely*.

5. tossing an even number or an odd number ______________
6. tossing an even number or a number less than 3 ______________
7. tossing a factor of 4 or a factor of 6 ______________
8. tossing a multiple of 2 or a multiple of 3 ______________

Name ______________________ Date ______________

Number and Operations

For 1–10, use a set of Cuisenaire® Rods.

1. Which rod is equivalent to $\frac{1}{2}$ of an orange rod? __________
2. Which rod is equivalent to $\frac{1}{3}$ of a blue rod? __________
3. Which rod is equivalent to $\frac{1}{4}$ of a brown rod? __________
4. Which rod is equivalent to $\frac{2}{3}$ of a blue rod? __________
5. Which rod is equivalent to $\frac{1}{8}$ of a brown rod? __________
6. Which rod is equivalent to $\frac{2}{4}$ of a brown rod? __________
7. Which rod is equivalent to $\frac{3}{10}$ of an orange rod? __________
8. Which rod is equivalent to $\frac{4}{5}$ of an orange rod? __________
9. Which rod is equivalent to $\frac{3}{4}$ of a brown rod? __________
10. Which rod is equivalent to $\frac{2}{3}$ of a dark green rod? __________

Problem Solving

Solve the problem. Explain your answer.

11. It takes the school cafeteria staff 10 minutes to make 25 lunches. They begin to prepare lunches at 10:15 A.M. and they have 200 lunches to prepare. At what time will they finish?

____

____

____

Name ______________________ Date ____________

Spiral Review
Lesson 4

Algebra

Write the rule that was used to find the numbers in the bottom row from the numbers in the top row. Then fill in the missing numbers.

1.

2	7	4	6	12	5	
8	28	16	24	48		36

____

2.

12	6	24	30	18		27
4		8		6	5	

____

3.

6	15	9	21	13		34
13	22	16	28		19	

____

Data Analysis and Probability

For 4–8, use the graph. No student represented has more than one pet.

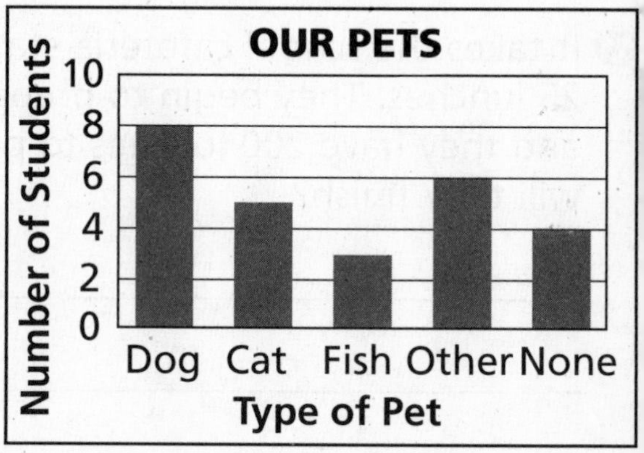

4. How many students do NOT have dogs, cats, or fish? ______________

5. How much greater is the number of students who have pets than the number who do not have pets?

____

6. How much greater is the number of students who have a pet that is not a dog than the number who have a dog? ______________

7. What fraction of the students have either a dog or a cat? ______________

Name ______________________ Date ____________

Spiral Review
Lesson 5

Number and Operations

Fill in the empty frames to complete the multiplication.

1. 27 × 18

×	20	7	27
10	200	70	
8	160	56	
18			

2. 25 × 23

×	20	5	25
20	400	100	
3	60	15	
23			

3. 32 × 24

×	30	2	32
20			
4			
24			

4. 17 × 34

×	10	7	17
30			
4			
34			

5. 36 × 21

×	30	6	36
20			
1			
21			

6. 42 × 16

×	40	2	42
10			
6			
16			

Measurement

Write the equivalent measure.

7. 2 quarts = ______ gallon
8. 6 cups = ______ quarts
9. 12 cups = ______ quarts
10. 1 gallon = ______ pints
11. 2 quarts = ______ cups
12. 8 pints = ______ cups
13. 3 gallons = ______ quarts
14. 2 pints = ______ cups
15. 16 quarts = ______ pints
16. 16 cups = ______ gallon
17. 2 gallons = ______ cups
18. 12 cups = ______ pints

Name ______________________ Date ______________

Spiral Review
Lesson 6

Geometry

Write *acute, right,* or *obtuse* to describe the angle.

1. 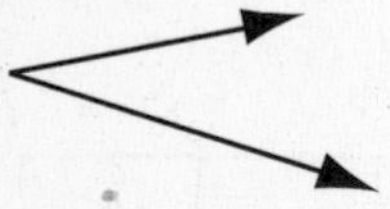

____

2. 

____

3. 

____

4. 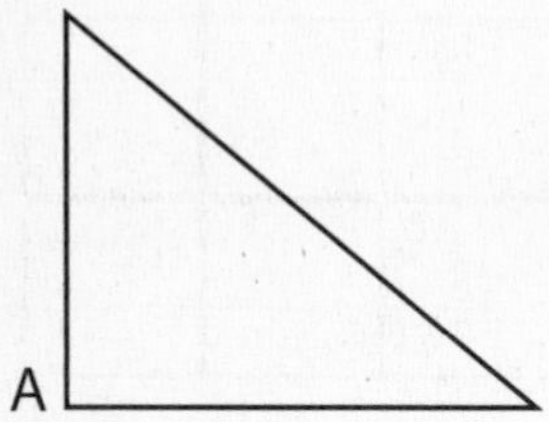

____

5. 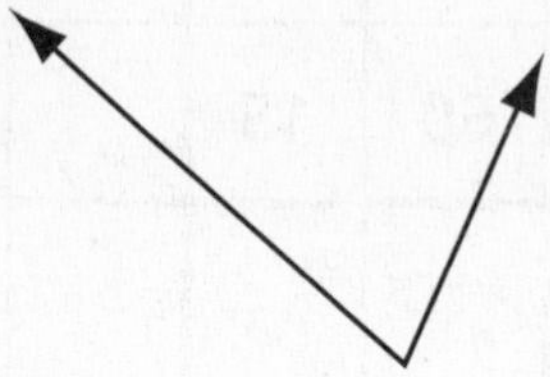

____

6. 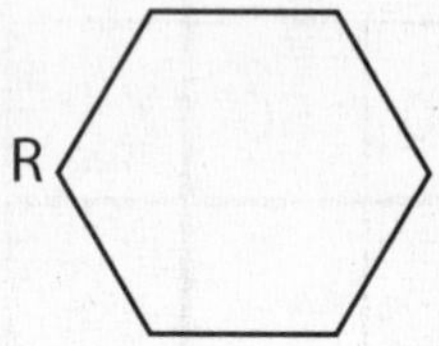

____

7. 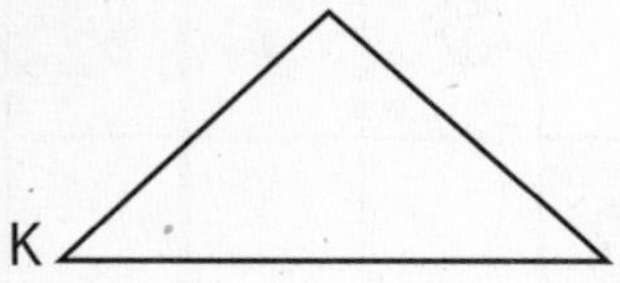

____

8. 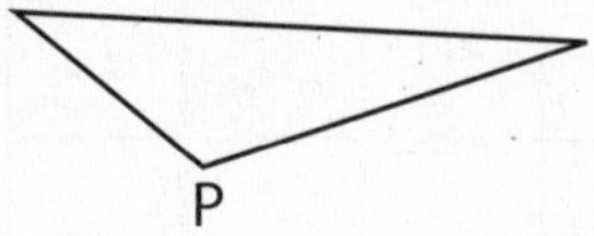

____

9. 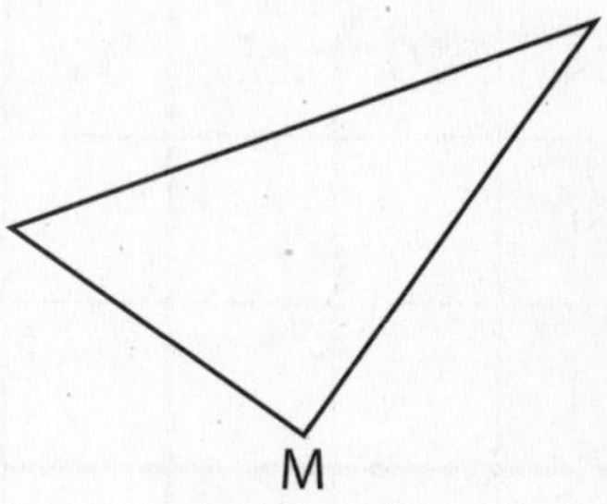

____

Problem Solving

Solve the problem. Explain your answer.

10. Jake has a fair spinner numbered 1–8. He spins it 24 times to see how many numbers come up exactly $\frac{1}{8}$ of the time. Here are his results.

3, 4, 4, 5, 6, 8, 7, 1, 8, 7, 3, 2, 5, 5, 4, 6, 7, 1, 2, 3, 8, 2, 5, 7

Which numbers came up more times than expected?

____

____

____

Name ______________________ Date ____________

Spiral Review
Lesson 1

Number and Operations

Write the value of the underlined digit.

1. 59<u>4</u>,305 ________
2. <u>8</u>3,912 ________
3. <u>7</u>08,346 ________
4. 9<u>9</u>2,025 ________
5. <u>4</u>,032,669 ________

Write the number described.

6. 10,000 more than 305,018 ________
7. 100,000 less than 1,823,208 ________
8. 1,000 more than 992,745 ________
9. 1,000,000 less than 3,049,627 ________
10. 100,000 more than 971,307 ________
11. 10,000 less than 230,475 ________
12. 100,000 less than 1,032,308 ________

Geometry

Write *prism* or *pyramid* to describe the figure. If the figure is neither a prism nor a pyramid, write *neither*.

13. 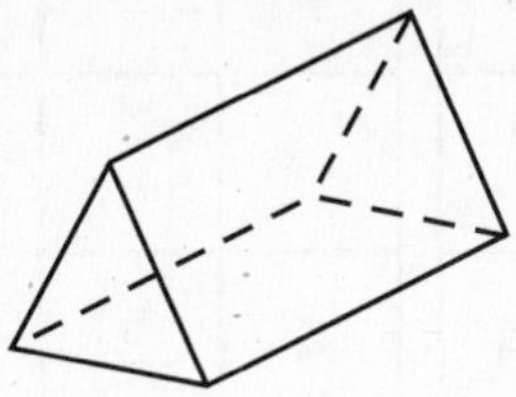

____

14. 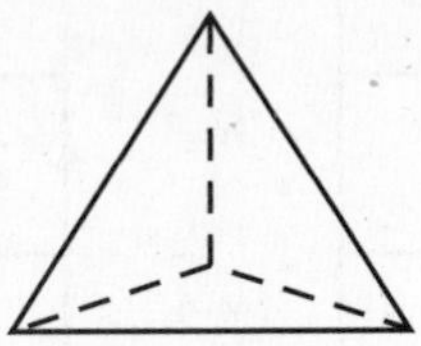

____

15. 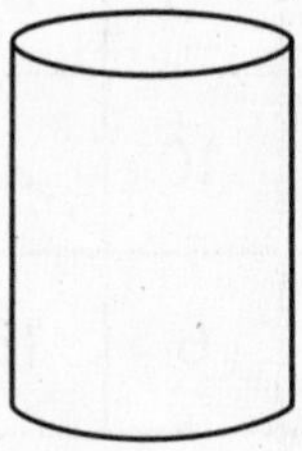

____

Name ______________________ Date ______________

Data Analysis and Probability

For 1–5, use the cards. A card is picked and replaced 20 times. Predict the number of times the result will occur. Explain your prediction.

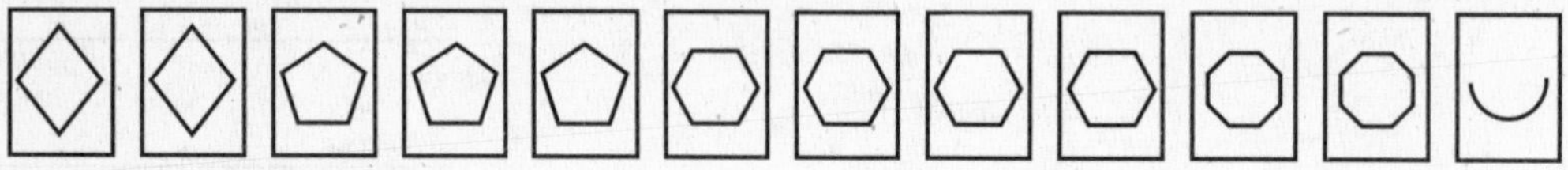

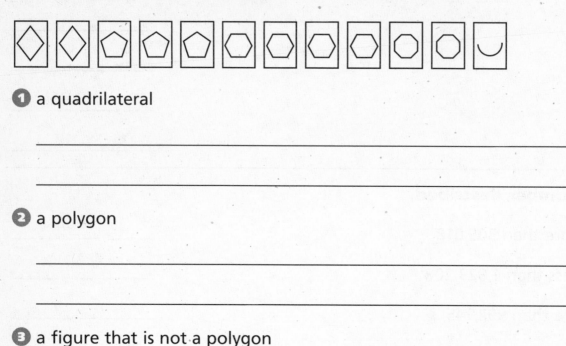

1. a quadrilateral

____

____

2. a polygon

____

____

3. a figure that is not a polygon

____

____

Reasoning and Proof

Study the first magic square. Describe the pattern that was used to make the second magic square. Then complete the second magic square.

4.

4	14	12
18	10	2
8	6	16

9	29	25
37		
17		

____

5.

6	21	18
27	15	3
12	9	24

		6
		1
4	3	8

____

Name ______________________ Date ____________

Spiral Review
Lesson 3

Measurement

Complete the statement with *grams* or *kilograms*.

1. A coffee pot might weigh about 1,000 ____________.
2. A classroom desk might weigh about 10 ____________.
3. A stapler might weigh about 200 ____________.
4. A car might weigh about 1,500 ____________.

Write the weights in order from least to greatest.

5. 120 grams, 1 kilogram, 900 grams

____

6. 2.5 kilograms, 3,000 grams, 2,200 grams

____

Problem Solving

Solve the problem. Explain your answer.

7. The school librarian opens a carton of 30 new books. He puts half of them on the shelf and gives $\frac{1}{3}$ of the rest to a teacher. How many books remain in the carton?

____

____

____

8. Heather has 20 math homework problems. She does $\frac{1}{4}$ of them right after she gets home from school and $\frac{1}{5}$ of the remaining ones right before dinner. How many problems does she have to do after dinner?

____

____

Name ______________________ Date ____________

Algebra

Write the missing numbers in the number sentences.

1. $9 \times \square = 18$ $18 \div 9 = \square$	2. $7 \times \square = 42$ $42 \div 7 = \square$	3. $\square \times 9 = 36$ $36 \div 9 = \square$
4. $4 \times \square = 32$ $32 \div \square = 4$	5. $8 \times \square = 48$ $48 \div \square = 6$	6. $35 \div \square = 7$ $5 \times \square = 35$
7. $54 \div 9 = \square$ $\square \times 9 = 54$	8. $81 \div 9 = \square$ $9 \times \square = 81$	9. $9 \times 7 = \square$ $\square \div 7 = 9$

Geometry

Find the volume of the prism.

10.
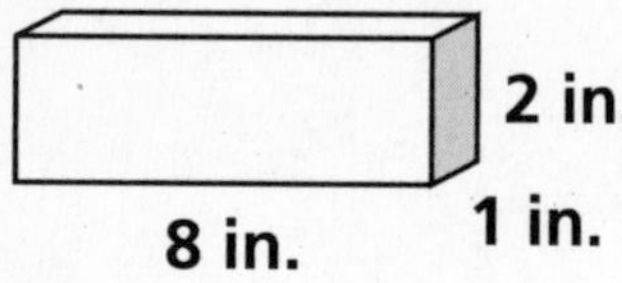

____

11.
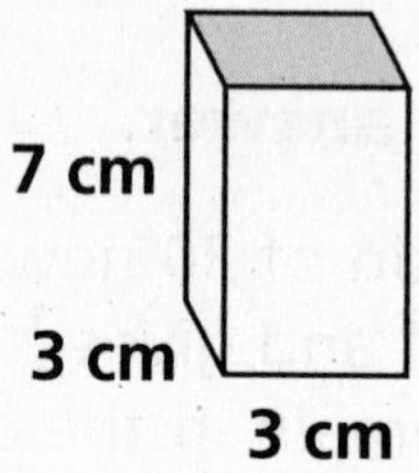

____

12.
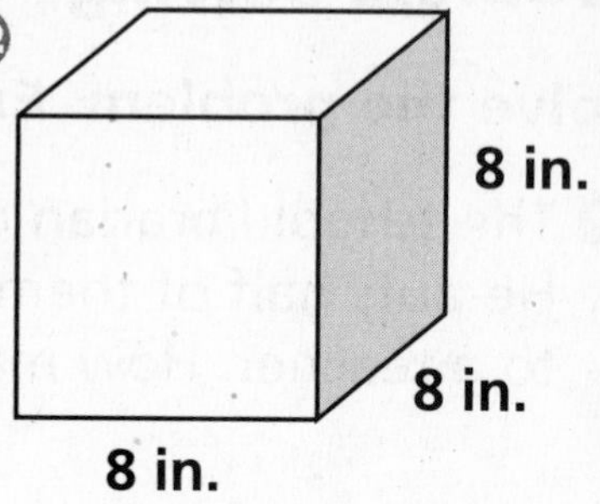

____

13.
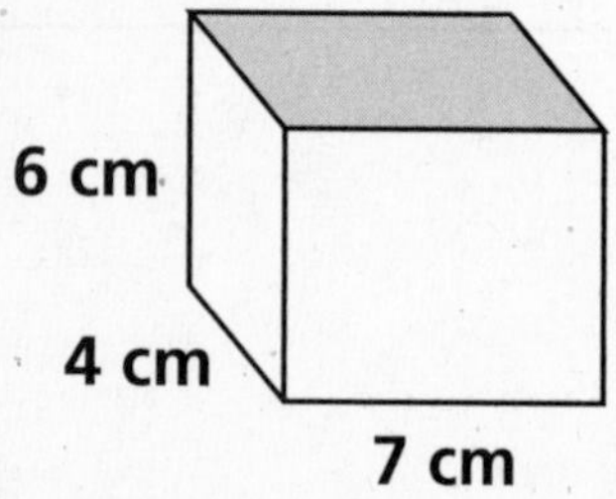

____

14.
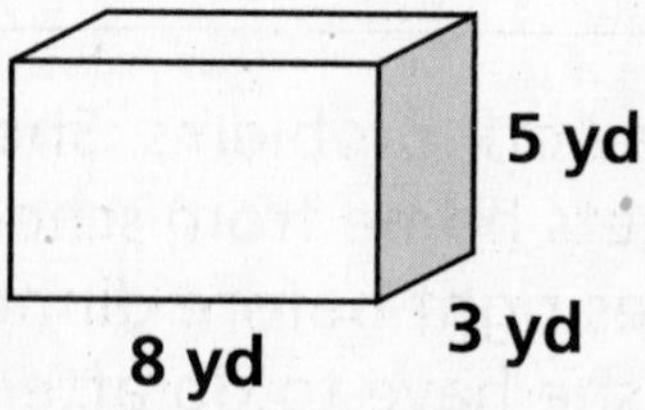

____

15.
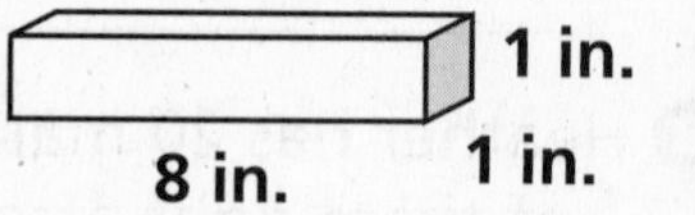

____

Name ______________________________ Date ______________

Spiral Review
Lesson 5

Number and Operations

Use the expression to solve the problem.

1. Jason trains for a bicycle race by biking 25 miles per day for 25 days. How far does he bike during that time?

   $(25 \times 20) + (25 \times 5) =$ __________ miles

2. A shipment of cans of corn has 22 cartons with 24 cans in each carton. How many cans are in the shipment?

   $(20 \times 24) + (2 \times 24) =$ __________ cans

3. Five friends each order the same breakfast. The cost for each friend is \$3.95. How much do they spend in all?

   $(5 \times \$4.00) - (5 \times \$0.05) = \$$ __________

Geometry

Write *acute, right,* or *obtuse* to describe the triangle.

4. 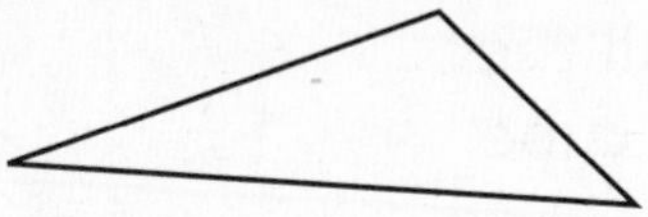

   ____

5. 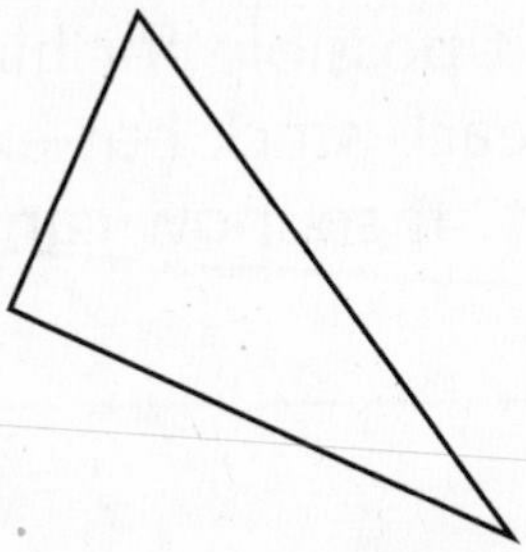

   ____

6. 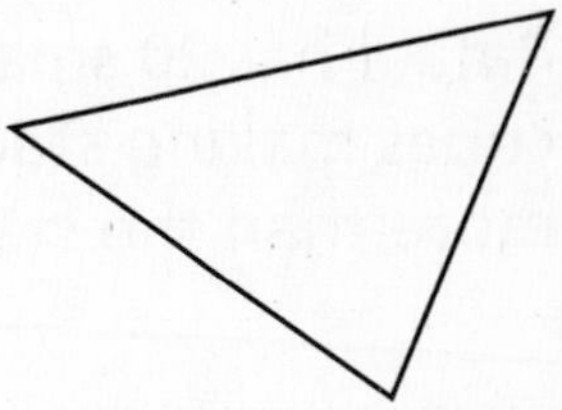

   ____

7.  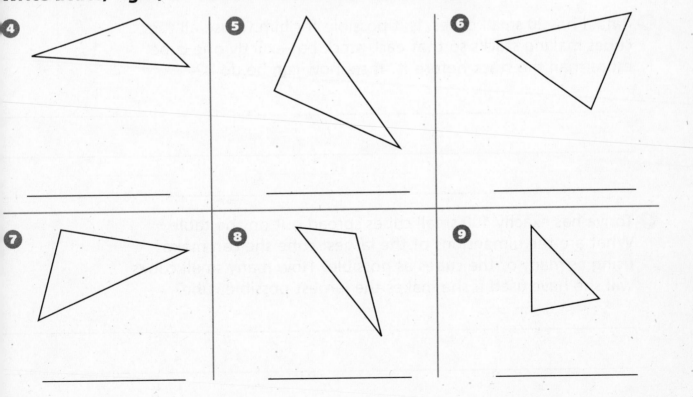

   ____

8. 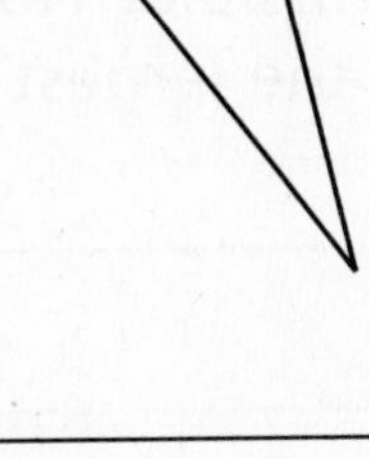

   ____

9. 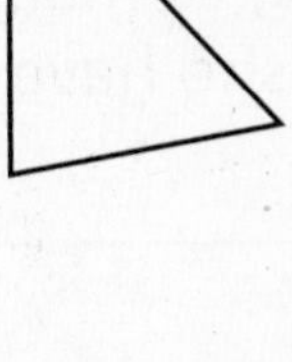

   ____

Name ______________________ Date ____________

Number and Operations

Write a decimal and a fraction to represent each part of the grid.

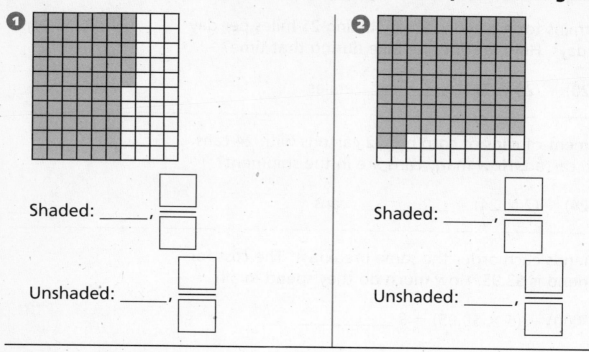

1

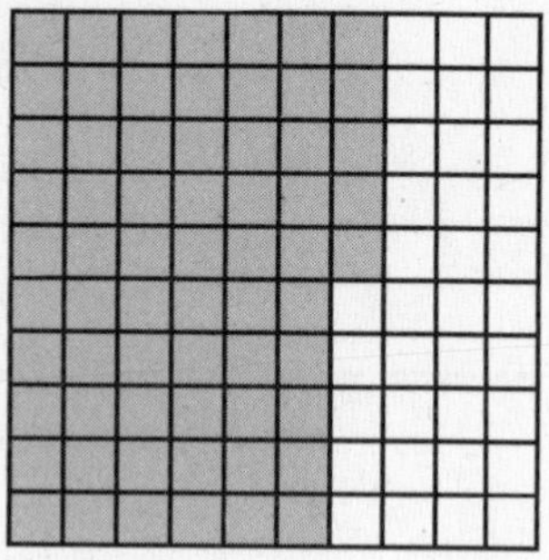

Shaded: ______, $\frac{\square}{\square}$

Unshaded: ______, $\frac{\square}{\square}$

2

Shaded: ______, $\frac{\square}{\square}$

Unshaded: ______, $\frac{\square}{\square}$

Problem Solving

Solve the problem. Explain your answer.

3 Rafael has 20 small cubes. Is it possible for him to use all the cubes making stacks so that each stack has exactly one cube more than the stack before it? If so, how can he do it?

____

____

____

4 Tonya has exactly 100 small cubes spread out on the table. What are the dimensions of the largest cube she can make using as many of the cubes as possible? How many small cubes will she have used if she makes the largest possible cube?

____

____

Name ______________________ Date ______________

Spiral Review
Lesson 7

Measurement

Complete the number sentence.

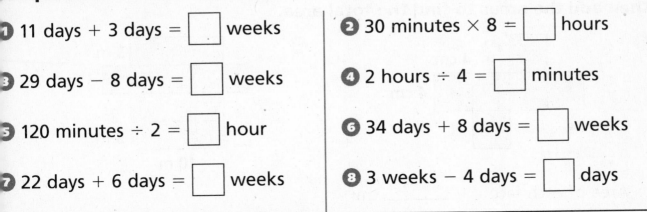

1. 11 days + 3 days = ☐ weeks
2. 30 minutes × 8 = ☐ hours
3. 29 days − 8 days = ☐ weeks
4. 2 hours ÷ 4 = ☐ minutes
5. 120 minutes ÷ 2 = ☐ hour
6. 34 days + 8 days = ☐ weeks
7. 22 days + 6 days = ☐ weeks
8. 3 weeks − 4 days = ☐ days

Data Analysis and Probability

For 9–11, use either the survey data or the graph.

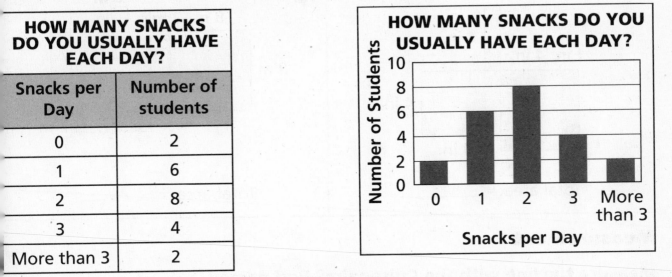

HOW MANY SNACKS DO YOU USUALLY HAVE EACH DAY?

Snacks per Day	Number of students
0	2
1	6
2	8
3	4
More than 3	2

HOW MANY SNACKS DO YOU USUALLY HAVE EACH DAY?

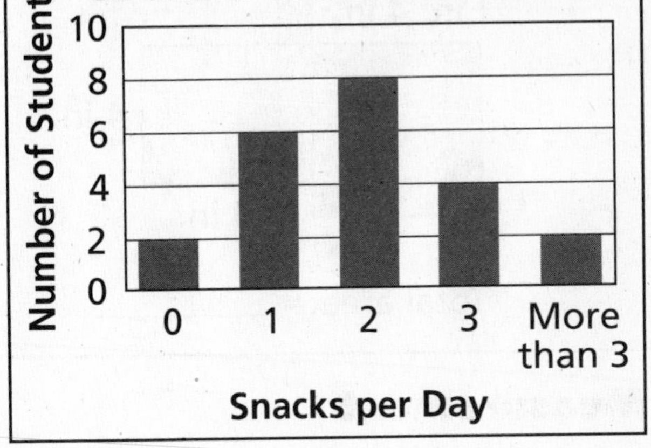

9. How many students answered the question? ______________

10. What was the most common response? ______________

11. How would you describe the pattern shown in the graph?

____

____

____

Name ______________________ Date ____________

Geometry

Find the area of each face of the figure. Then add the areas to find the total area.

1.

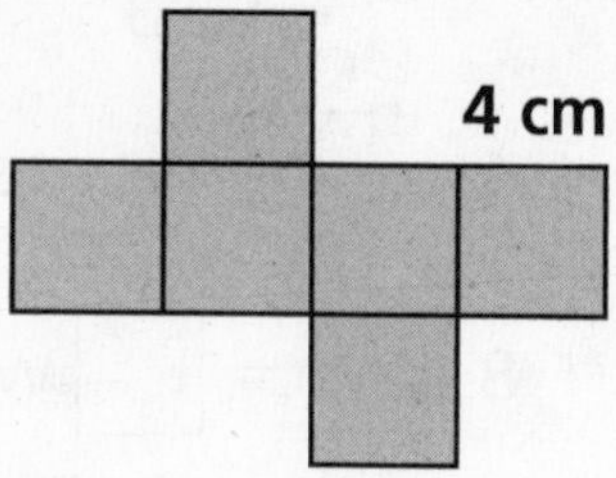

Area of each face = ________ cm^2

Total area = ________ cm^2

2.

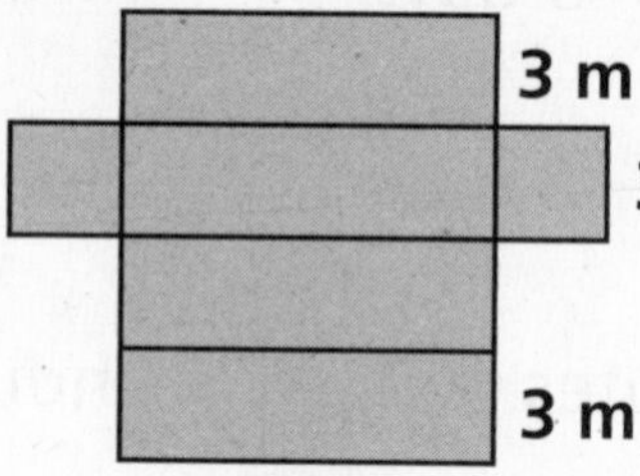

Total area = ________

3.

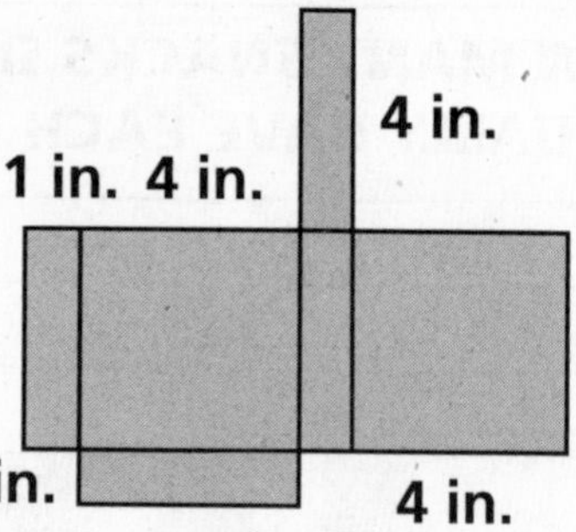

Total area = ________

4.

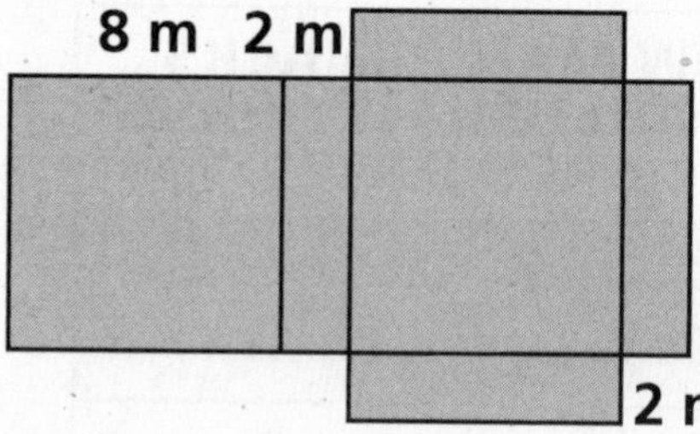

Total area = ________

Measurement

Measure the line with the Cuisenaire® Rod named. Then write the length of the line in centimeters.

5. white ☐ cm

6. purple ☐ cm

7. yellow ☐ cm

Name ______________________ Date ____________

Spiral Review
Lesson 2

Number and Operations

Fill in the missing numbers on the number line.

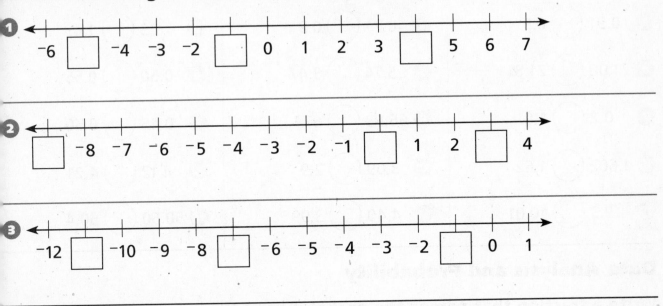

1. −6, ☐, −4, −3, −2, ☐, 0, 1, 2, 3, ☐, 5, 6, 7

2. ☐, −8, −7, −6, −5, −4, −3, −2, −1, ☐, 1, 2, ☐, 4

3. −12, ☐, −10, −9, −8, ☐, −6, −5, −4, −3, −2, ☐, 0, 1

Problem Solving

Solve the problem. Explain your answer.

Antonio asked his classmates to name their favorite after-school activity. Here are the results.

play sports	play a game	play sports	watch TV	play a game
watch TV	play a game	watch TV	play sports	play a game
play a game	read	play a game	play a game	play a game
watch TV	read	play sports	play a game	do homework
play sports	play a game	read	read	play sports

____

____

____

Name ________________________ Date ______________

Number and Operations

Write > or < to compare the numbers.

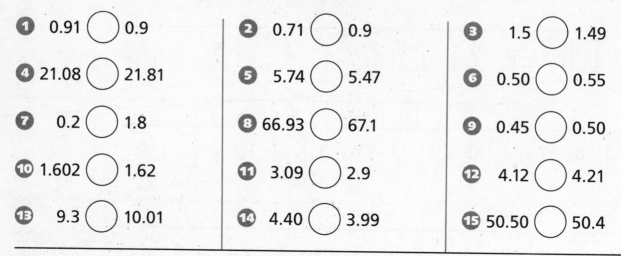

1. 0.91 ◯ 0.9	2. 0.71 ◯ 0.9	3. 1.5 ◯ 1.49
4. 21.08 ◯ 21.81	5. 5.74 ◯ 5.47	6. 0.50 ◯ 0.55
7. 0.2 ◯ 1.8	8. 66.93 ◯ 67.1	9. 0.45 ◯ 0.50
10. 1.602 ◯ 1.62	11. 3.09 ◯ 2.9	12. 4.12 ◯ 4.21
13. 9.3 ◯ 10.01	14. 4.40 ◯ 3.99	15. 50.50 ◯ 50.4

Data Analysis and Probability

Write a fraction that names the probability of the event.

Roll a 1–6 number cube.

16. an even number ☐
17. a number less than 3 ☐
18. a multiple of 4 ☐
19. a number greater than 5 ☐

Spin a spinner labeled A, B, C, D, E, F, G, H.

20. a vowel ☐
21. a consonant ☐
22. a letter from the word BAG ☐

Spin a spinner numbered 2–9.

23. an even number ☐
24. a number less than 3 ☐
25. a multiple of 3 ☐
26. a number greater than 6 ☐

Name ______________________________ Date ______________

Algebra

Complete the table for the number sentence $y = x + 3$. Then draw a graph of the relationship.

1

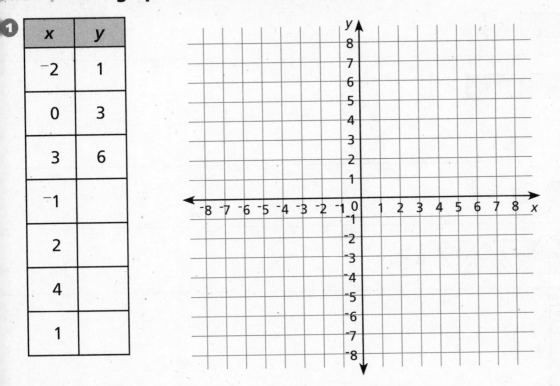

x	y
$^{-}2$	1
0	3
3	6
$^{-}1$	
2	
4	
1	

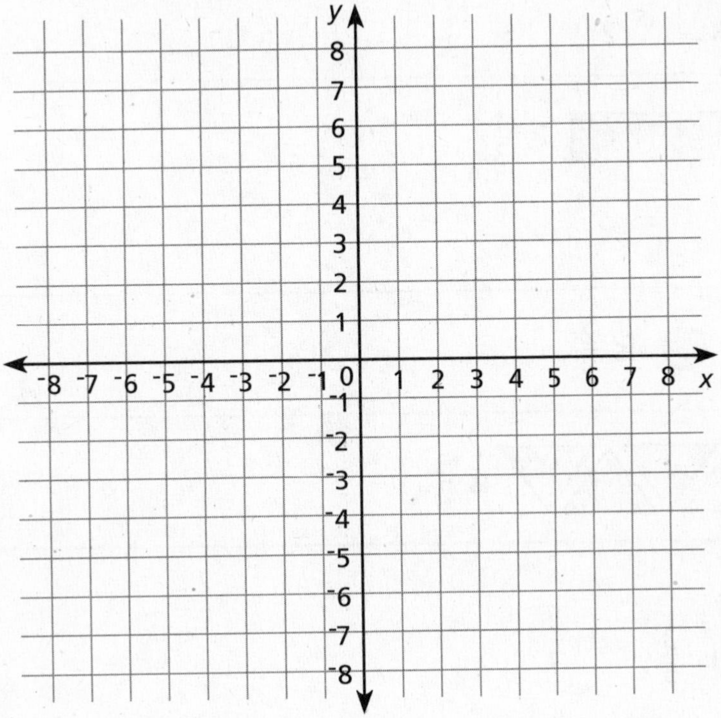

Geometry

Find the area of the figure. The area of the smallest square is 1 square centimeter.

2

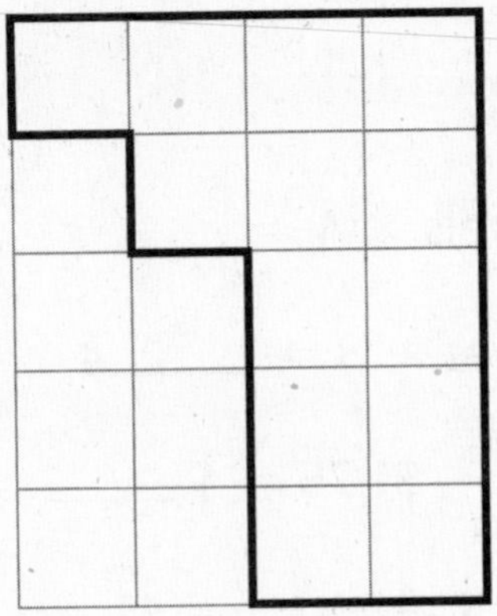

3

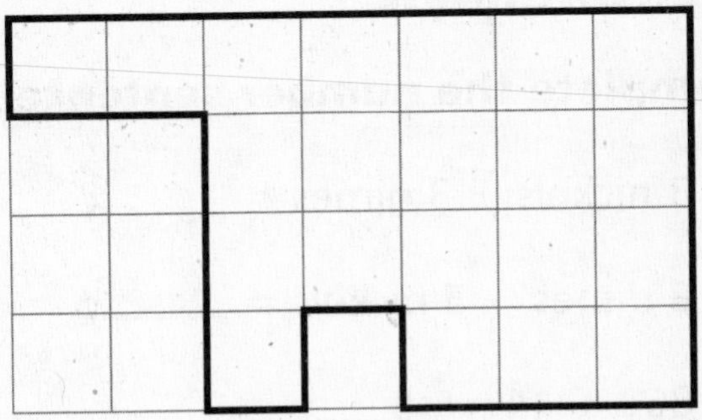

Name ______________________ Date ______________

Number and Operations

Draw the whole unit if the picture represents the fraction given.

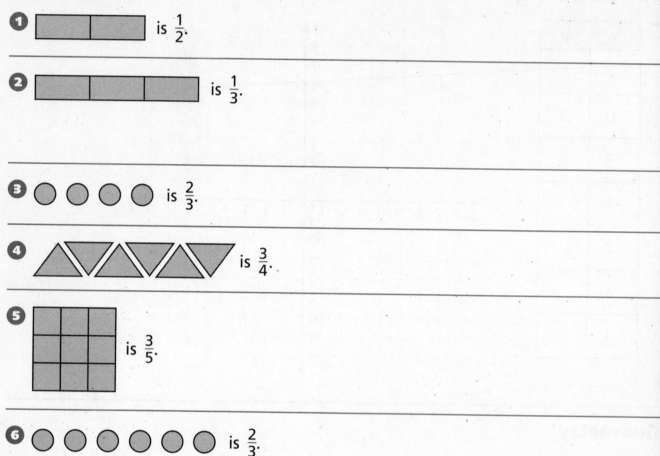

1. 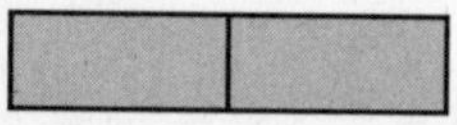 is $\frac{1}{2}$.

2.  is $\frac{1}{3}$.

3. 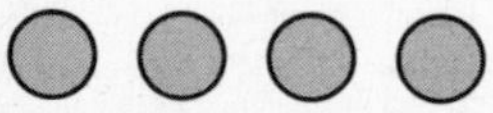 is $\frac{2}{3}$.

4.  is $\frac{3}{4}$.

5. 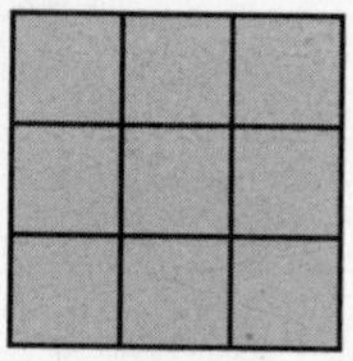 is $\frac{3}{5}$.

6. 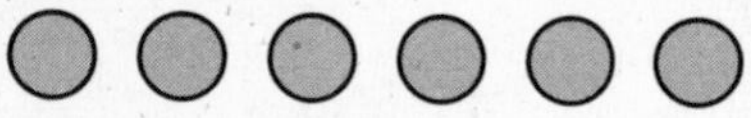 is $\frac{2}{3}$.

Measurement

Complete the number sentence.

7. 3 nickels + 3 dimes = ______¢

8. 2 nickels × 4 = ______¢

9. 8 dimes − 5 nickels = ______¢

10. 6 dimes ÷ 3 = ______¢

11. 86¢ + 14¢ = $______

12. $3.00 − $1.75 = $______

13. 15¢ × 4 = ______¢

14. $3.00 ÷ 4 = ______¢

15. $1.75 + $2.50 = $______

16. 25¢ × 6 = $______

17. $4.25 − $2.00 = $______

18. 71¢ − 24¢ = ______¢

Name ______________________ Date ____________

Data Analysis and Probability

For 1–4, use the bar graph.

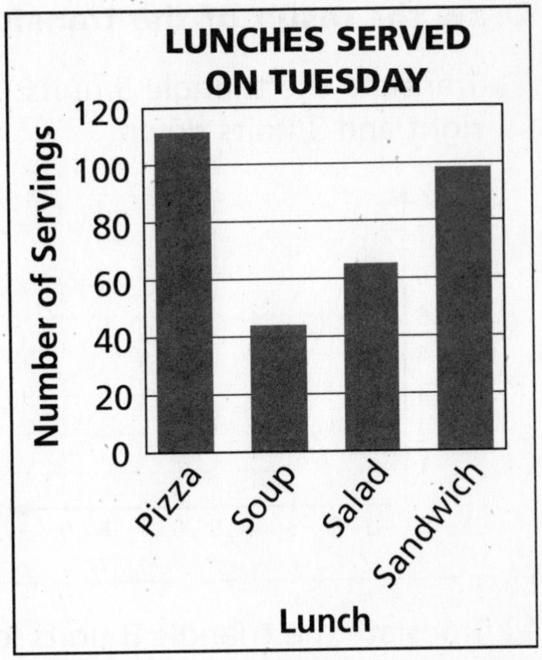

1. Which was the most popular lunch served on Tuesday?

   ____

2. Which two types of lunches together were the closest to 100 lunches?

   ____

3. About how many more sandwiches were served than salads?

   ____

4. Estimate the number of lunches that were served on Tuesday. ______________________

5. Which two types of lunches were the closest in the number served? ______________________

Problem Solving

Solve the problem. Explain your answer.

6. Sol built a fence around his square garden. He used 8 fence posts on each side, including 1 at each corner. How many posts did he use in all?

   ____

   ____

   ____

   ____

   ____

Name ______________________ Date ______________

Geometry

Draw the result of the transformation.

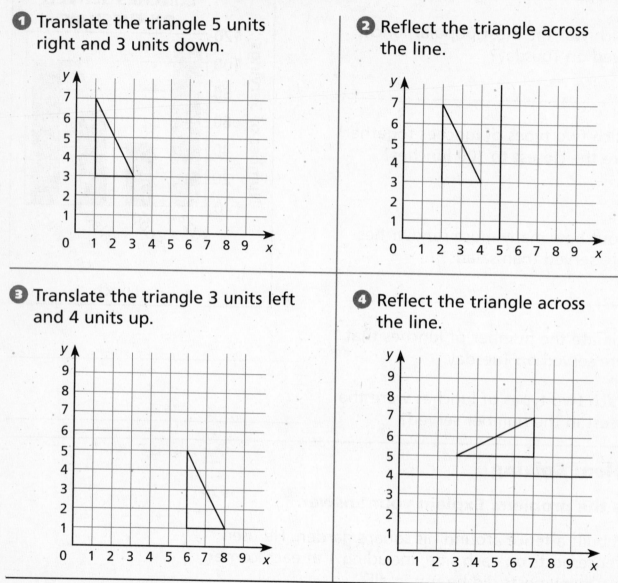

1 Translate the triangle 5 units right and 3 units down.

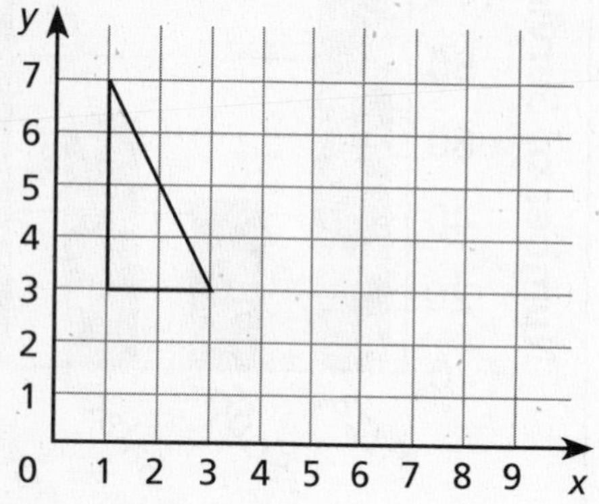

2 Reflect the triangle across the line.

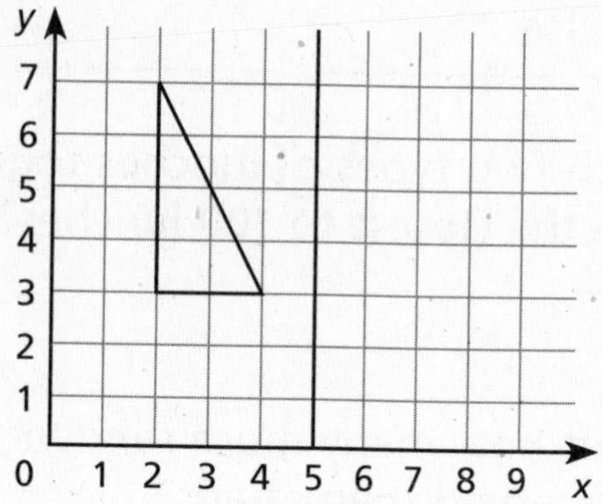

3 Translate the triangle 3 units left and 4 units up.

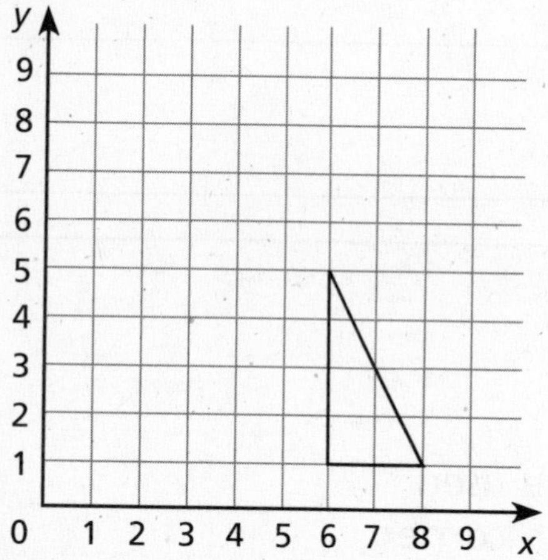

4 Reflect the triangle across the line.

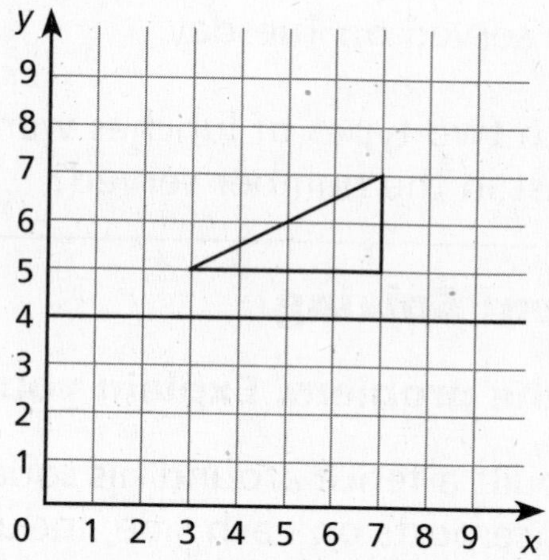

Problem Solving

Solve the problem. Explain your answer.

5 How many different money amounts can you make with a penny, a nickel, a dime, and a quarter?

____

____

Name ______________________ Date ____________

Spiral Review
Lesson 2

Number and Operations

Complete the fact family for the area of the rectangle.

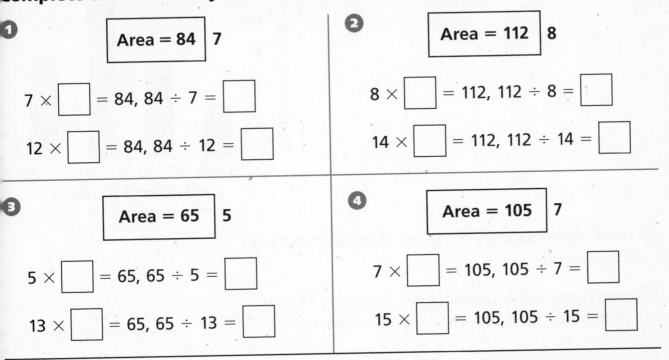

1. Area = 84 | 7

7 × ☐ = 84, 84 ÷ 7 = ☐

12 × ☐ = 84, 84 ÷ 12 = ☐

2. Area = 112 | 8

8 × ☐ = 112, 112 ÷ 8 = ☐

14 × ☐ = 112, 112 ÷ 14 = ☐

3. Area = 65 | 5

5 × ☐ = 65, 65 ÷ 5 = ☐

13 × ☐ = 65, 65 ÷ 13 = ☐

4. Area = 105 | 7

7 × ☐ = 105, 105 ÷ 7 = ☐

15 × ☐ = 105, 105 ÷ 15 = ☐

Measurement

For 5–8, use the table.

	Temperature at 9:00 A.M.	Temperature at noon	Temperature at 6:00 P.M.
Saturday	47°F	61°F	56°F
Sunday	43°F	49°F	45°F
Monday	38°F	52°F	43°F

5. On which day was there the greatest change in temperatures between 9:00 A.M. and 6:00 P.M.? ____________

6. On what day and time was the warmest temperature measured? ____________

7. Which day had the least change in temperature between 9:00 A.M. and noon? ____________

8. By how many degrees did the temperature change on Monday from 9:00 A.M. to noon? ____________

Name ______________________ Date ____________

Data Analysis and Probability

For 1–5, use the histogram.

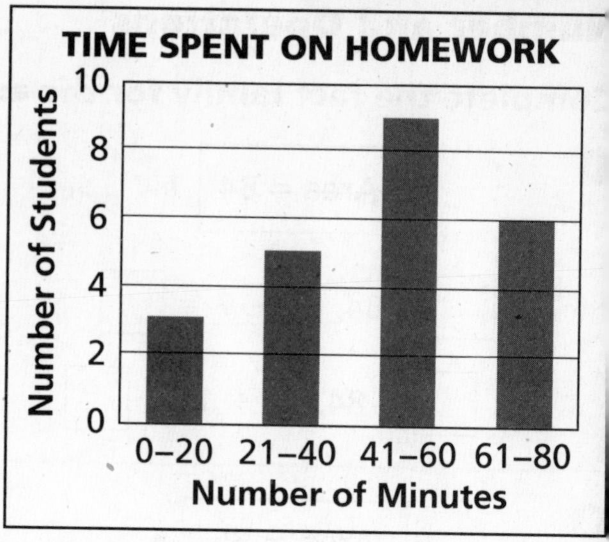

1. How many students did more than 40 minutes of homework? ____________
2. How many more students did between 21 and 40 minutes than between 0 and 20 minutes? ____________
3. How many students are included in the graph's data? ____________
4. How many students did 1 hour or less of homework? ____________
5. Did more students do less than 41 minutes or more than 1 hour of homework? How many more students? ____________

Problem Solving

Solve the problem. Explain your answer.

6. The Shirt Shop has 125 shirts left after a busy Saturday. They sold shirts to 48 customers. Of those customers, 29 bought one shirt, 12 bought 2 shirts, and the rest bought 3 shirts. How many shirts did the Shirt Shop have at the start of the day?

____

____

____

Name ________________________ Date ____________

Spiral Review
Lesson 4

Number and Operations

Find the quotient.

1. $6\overline{)270}$	2. $5\overline{)480}$	3. $4\overline{)292}$	4. $7\overline{)406}$
5. $15\overline{)165}$	6. $12\overline{)228}$	7. $3\overline{)381}$	8. $8\overline{)696}$
9. $9\overline{)441}$	10. $6\overline{)582}$	11. $8\overline{)512}$	12. $7\overline{)567}$

Geometry

Draw as many rectangles as you can with the given perimeter.

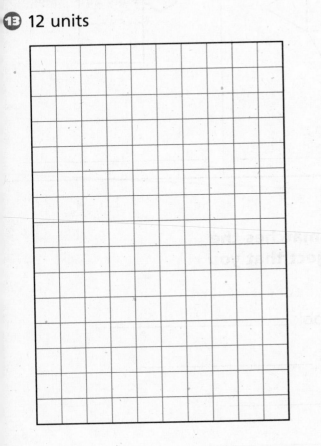

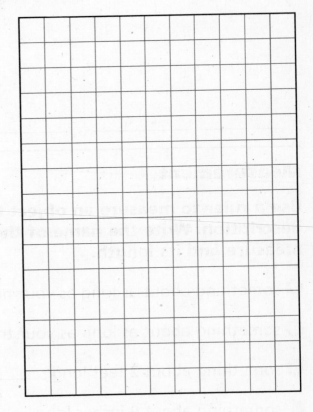

13. 12 units

14. 20 units

Name ______________________ Date ____________

Geometry

Describe the figure that can be made from the net.

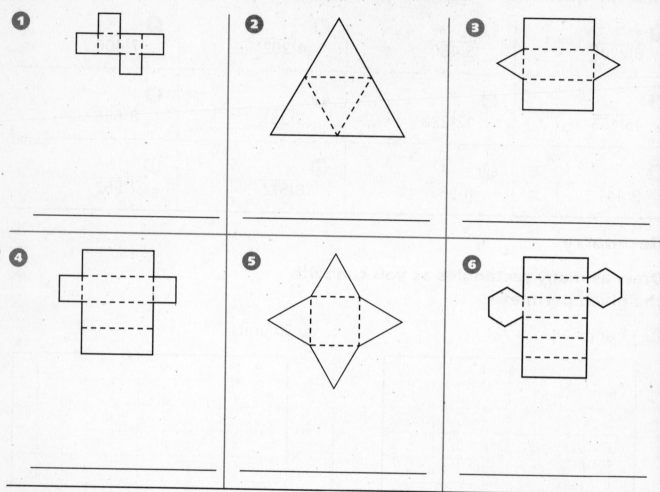

1 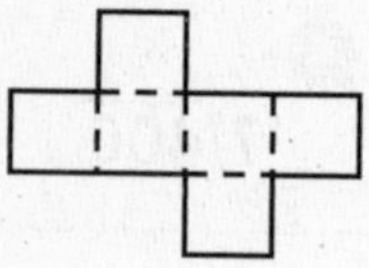

____

2 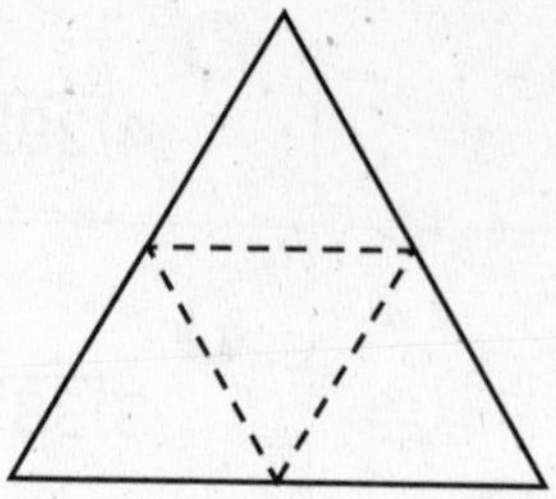

____

3 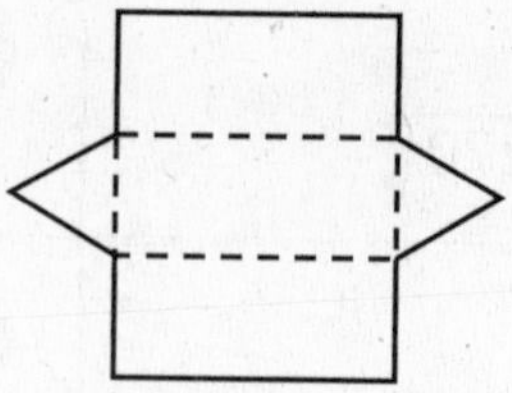

____

4 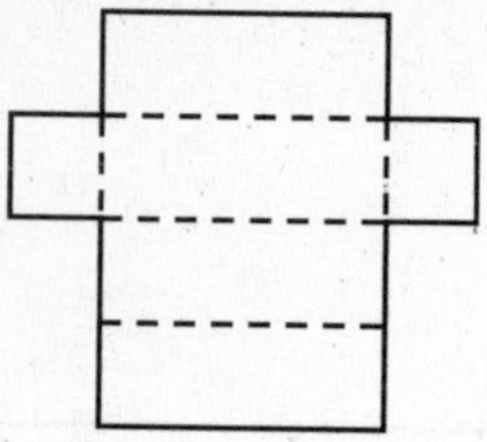

____

5 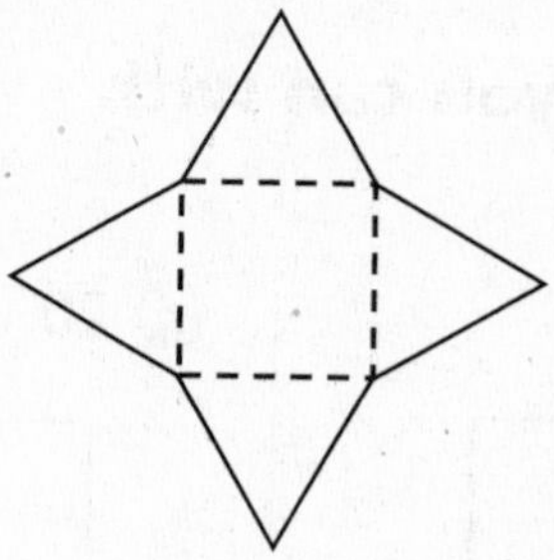

____

6 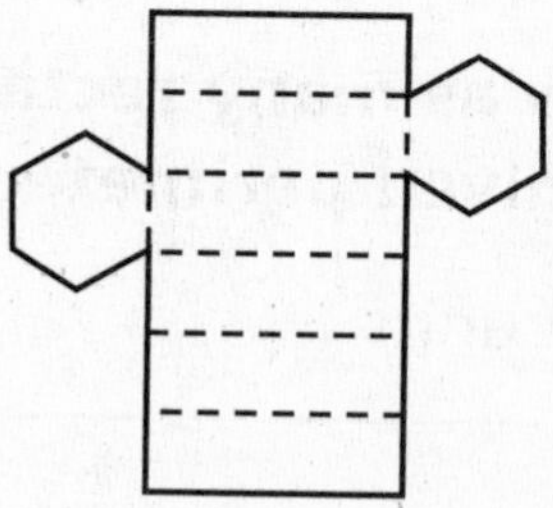

____

Measurement

Use a ruler to measure an object that matches the description. Write the name of the object that you measure and its length.

7 something about as long as your notebook _______________

8 something about as long as your thumb _______________

9 something about 2 feet long _______________

10 something about 9 inches long _______________

11 something about as tall as your teacher _______________

Name ______________________ Date ____________

Spiral Review
Lesson 6

Algebra

Complete the table.

	Write a number between 10 and 99.	Multiply the number by 9.	Add the digits in the product.
1			
2			
3			
4			
5			

6 Describe the pattern in the third column.

____

Data Analysis and Probability

For 7–11, write the numbers 1 through 10 on slips of paper. Predict how many times the outcome will occur for this experiment: Mix up the papers, pick one, record the number, and put the paper back. Do this 10 times. Write whether your results are close to your prediction.

7 a number less than 6 ______________

8 an odd number ______________

9 a multiple of 5 ______________

10 a 3 ______________

11 Why do you think the results might not match your predictions?

____

____

Name ______________________ Date ______________

Spiral Review
Lesson 1

Number and Operations

Use rounding or compatible numbers to estimate the missing factor or quotient.

1. $39 \times \square = 792$	2. $78\overline{)639}$	3. $18 \times \square = 379$
4. $6\overline{)532}$	5. $22\overline{)812}$	6. $51 \times \square = 486$
7. $37\overline{)1,835}$	8. $82 \times \square = 252$	9. $63 \times \square = 4,776$

Data Analysis and Probability

Write the probability as a fraction.

For 10–12, use this experiment: One card is picked from a deck of ten cards numbered 2 to 11.

10. an even numbered card ☐

11. a number that is a multiple of 3 ☐

12. a number that is a factor of 12 ☐

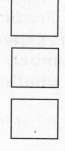

For 13–15, use this experiment: One marble is picked from a bag containing 5 red, 3 blue, 1 green, and 1 yellow.

13. a marble that is not red ☐

14. a marble that is either green or yellow ☐

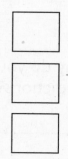

15. a marble that is not blue ☐

Name ______________________ Date ____________

Spiral Review
Lesson 2

Geometry

For 1–10, use the coordinate grid. Write an ordered pair to identify the location of each point.

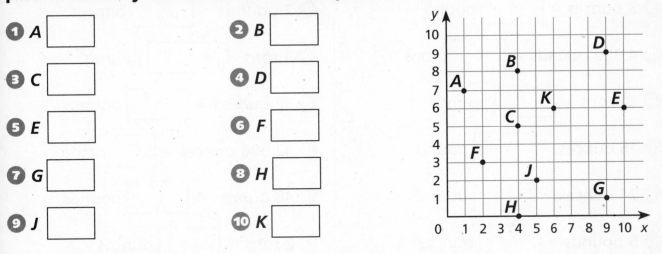

1. *A* ☐
2. *B* ☐
3. *C* ☐
4. *D* ☐
5. *E* ☐
6. *F* ☐
7. *G* ☐
8. *H* ☐
9. *J* ☐
10. *K* ☐

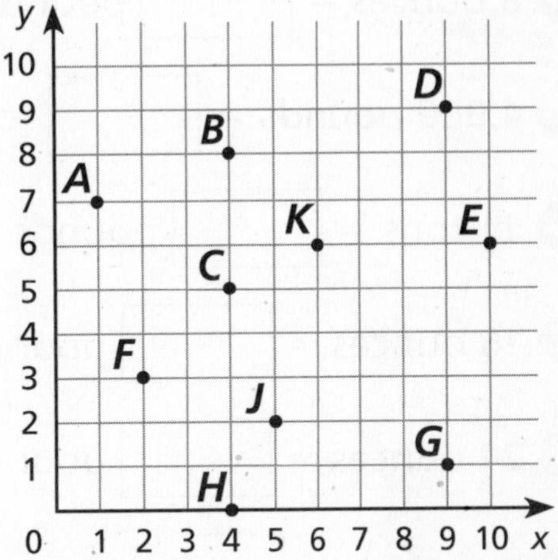

Reasoning and Proof

Follow the steps to complete the number puzzle.

Steps	Shorthand	11	12	13
Think of a number.	x			
Multiply by 2.	$2x$			
Add 3.	$2x + 3$			
Multiply by 2.	$4x + 6$			
Subtract 6.	$4x$			
Divide by 4.	x			

14. What do you notice about the answer in each puzzle?

____

Name ______________________ Date ____________

Measurement

Complete the equation.

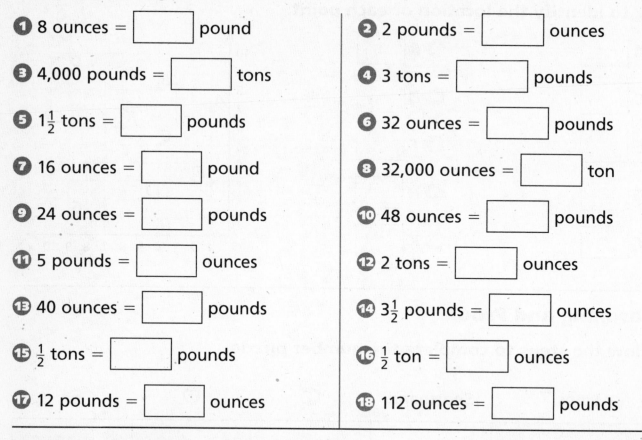

1. 8 ounces = ☐ pound
2. 2 pounds = ☐ ounces
3. 4,000 pounds = ☐ tons
4. 3 tons = ☐ pounds
5. $1\frac{1}{2}$ tons = ☐ pounds
6. 32 ounces = ☐ pounds
7. 16 ounces = ☐ pound
8. 32,000 ounces = ☐ ton
9. 24 ounces = ☐ pounds
10. 48 ounces = ☐ pounds
11. 5 pounds = ☐ ounces
12. 2 tons = ☐ ounces
13. 40 ounces = ☐ pounds
14. $3\frac{1}{2}$ pounds = ☐ ounces
15. $\frac{1}{2}$ tons = ☐ pounds
16. $\frac{1}{2}$ ton = ☐ ounces
17. 12 pounds = ☐ ounces
18. 112 ounces = ☐ pounds

Problem Solving

Solve the problem. Explain your answer.

19. Eric has two cubes, each the same size. He glues them together so that a face on one cube exactly matches a face on the other. How many faces does the new figure have?

____

____

20. Douglas puts a square tile on his desk. He places equilateral triangles around the square so that one side of each triangle touches one side of the square. How many sides does the new figure have?

____

____

Name ______________________ Date ______________

Spiral Review
Lesson 4

Algebra

Fill in the table. The first problem is done for you.

1.

x	4			
$3x + 4$	16	25	10	13

2.

x				
$2x - 7$	3	9	5	1

3.

x				
$4x - 1$	3	23	11	31

Data Analysis and Probability

For 4–7, use the bar graph.

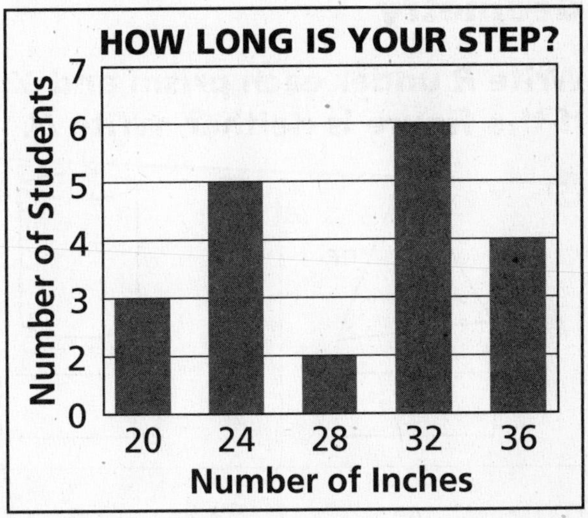

4. How many students have a step that is at least 28 inches long? ☐

5. How many students have a step that is no more than 28 inches? ☐

6. How many more students have a 32-inch step than a 20-inch step? ☐

7. There are 30 students in this class. How many are **not** represented in the graph? ☐

Name ______________________________ Date ______________

Spiral Review
Lesson 5

Number and Operations

Write < or > to compare the numbers.

1. 590,302 ◯ 590,320
2. 53,284 ◯ 53,199
3. 108,494 ◯ 180,001
4. 1,901,039 ◯ 1,901,093
5. 2,207,901 ◯ 2,207,190
6. 5,883,171 ◯ 5,838,992

Write the numbers in order from least to greatest.

7. 102,495 120,045 110,995 ______________________
8. 3,219,203 3,291,302 2,993,902 ______________________
9. 998,591 989,951 997,640 ______________________
10. 4,493,937 4,439,973 4,493,379 ______________________

Geometry

Write *R* under each prism and *Y* under each pyramid. If the figure is neither, write *N*.

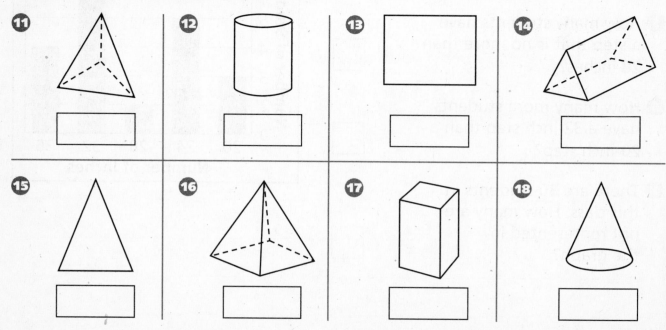

11. 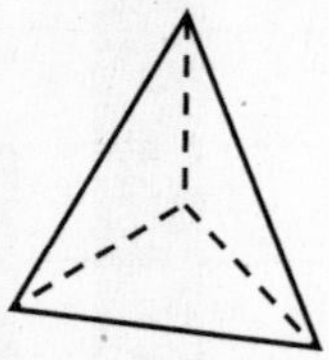
12. 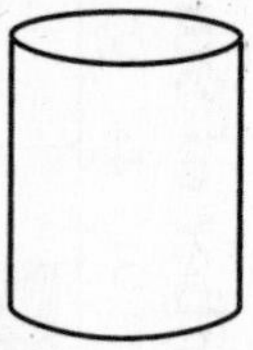
13. 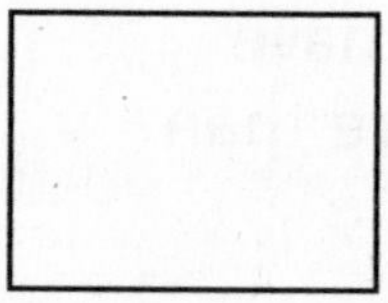
14. 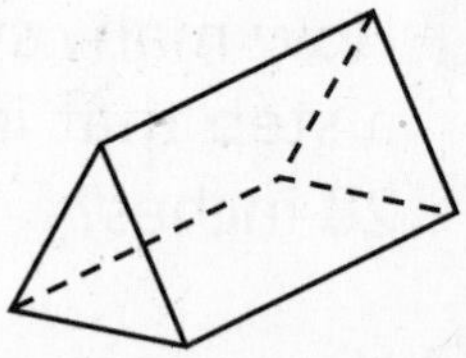
15. 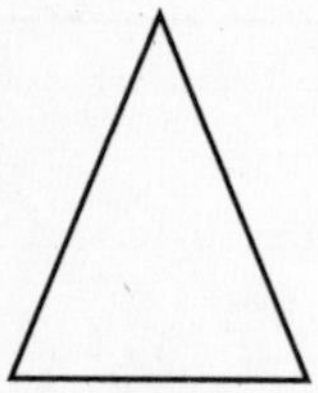
16. 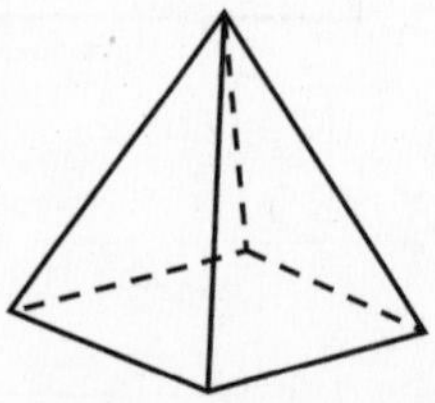
17. 
18. 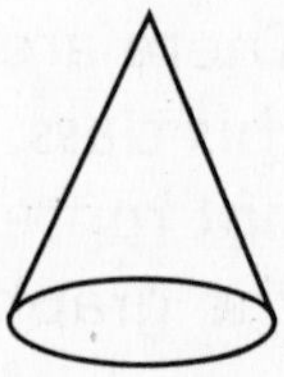

Name ______________________ Date ____________

Spiral Review
Lesson 6

Geometry

For 1–6, use the square shown at the right to find the perimeter and area. The square has a perimeter of 4 centimeters and an area of 1 square centimeter.

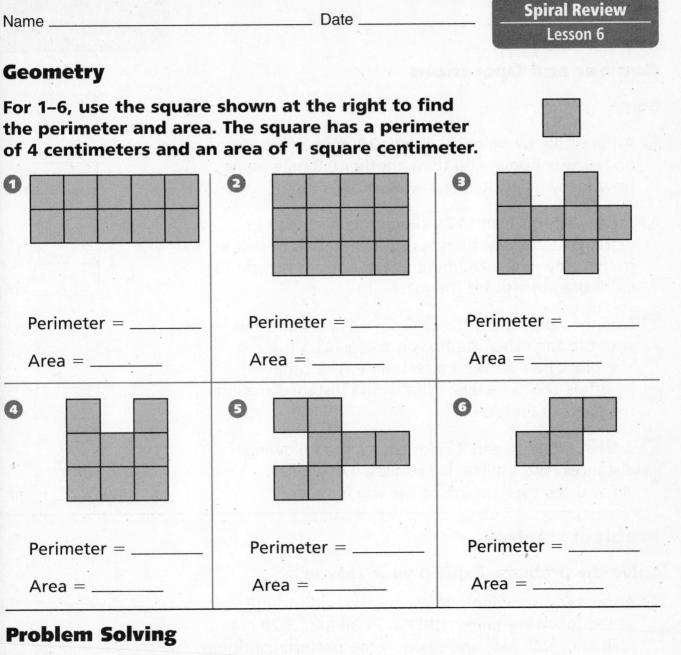

1. 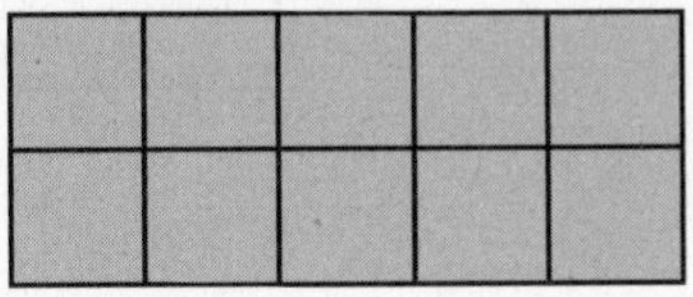

Perimeter = ________

Area = ________

2. 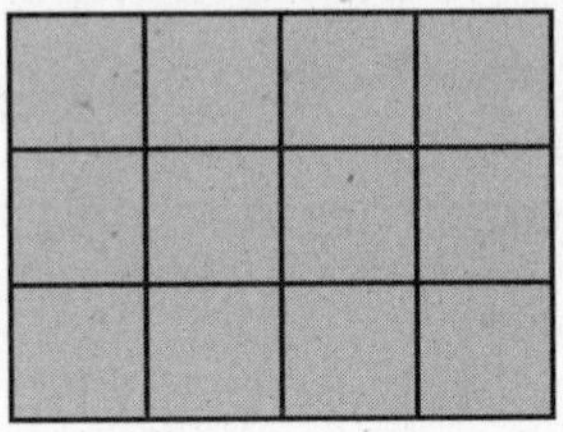

Perimeter = ________

Area = ________

3. 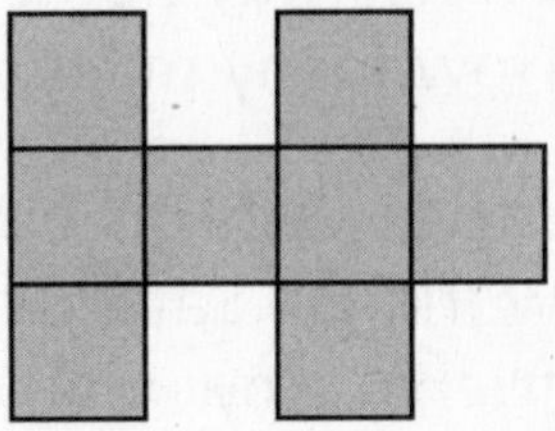

Perimeter = ________

Area = ________

4. 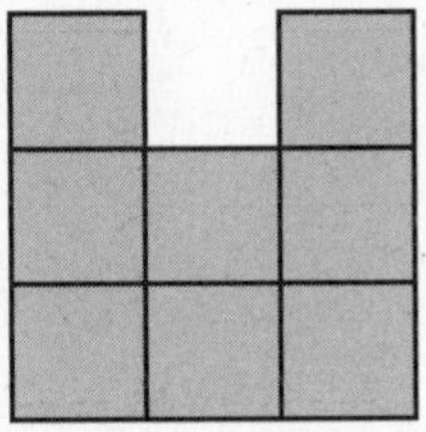

Perimeter = ________

Area = ________

5. 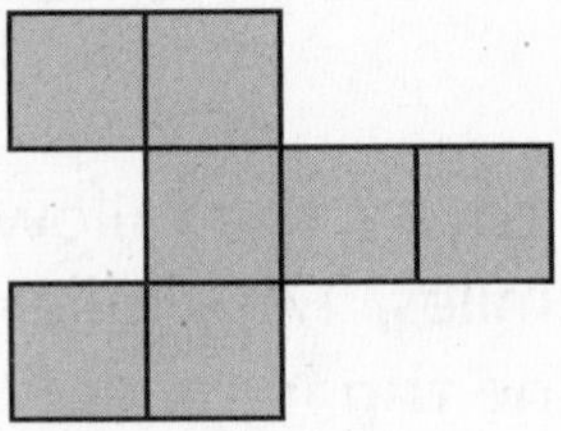

Perimeter = ________

Area = ________

6. 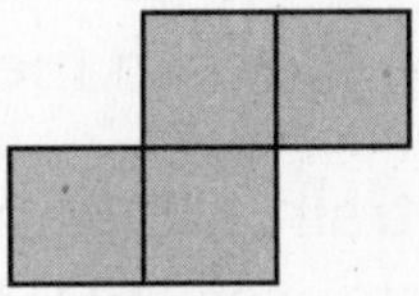

Perimeter = ________

Area = ________

Problem Solving

Solve the problem. Explain your answer.

7. Trisha's kitchen floor is 122 square feet. She buys 4 boxes of tiles. Each box covers 32 square feet. Does she have enough tiles for her floor? If not, how many more square feet of tiles does she need? If she has enough, how many extra square feet does she have?

____

____

____

____

Name ______________________ Date ______________

Number and Operations

Solve.

1. Anita walks 1.2 miles to school, 0.7 mile to the store on her way home, and then another 0.8 mile home. How many miles does she walk in all? ☐ mi

2. Javier rides his bike 13.25 kilometers each day to work. On Saturday, he rides 8.5 kilometers to visit a friend. How many kilometers farther does he ride to work than to visit his friend? ☐ km

3. Fred measures the distance from one corner of his street to the other. He finds it to be 142.5 meters. The block he lives on is a rectangle. The other length is 127.75 meters. What is the distance around the block in meters? ☐ m

4. A train trip between 3 cities covers the following distances: 192.3 miles, 187.6 miles, 179.9 miles. What is the total length of the trip in miles? ☐ mi

Problem solving

Solve the problem. Explain your answer.

5. A theater is showing a movie in two auditoriums at the following times: 1:10 P.M., 1:30 P.M., 3:20 P.M., 3:40 P.M., 5:30 P.M., and so on. If the pattern continues, at what time will the next show after 5:30 P.M. start?

____

____

6. In the pattern shown below, each number after the first two is found by adding the two numbers just before it. What are the next three numbers in the pattern?

   0, 3, 3, 6, 9, 15, 24, 39, ■, ■, ■

____

____

Name ________________________ Date ____________

Algebra

Find the products.

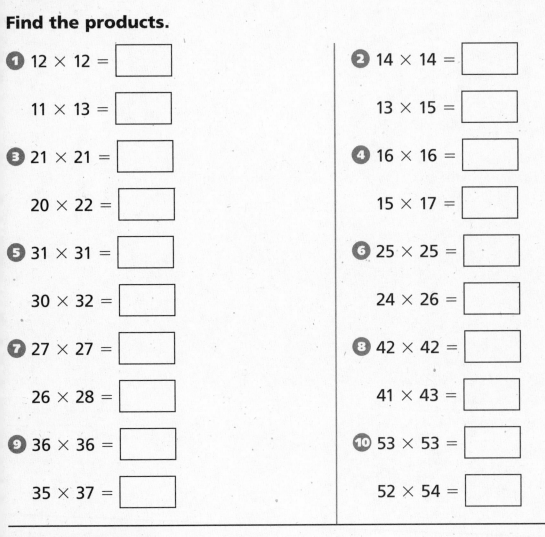

1. $12 \times 12 = \square$

   $11 \times 13 = \square$

2. $14 \times 14 = \square$

   $13 \times 15 = \square$

3. $21 \times 21 = \square$

   $20 \times 22 = \square$

4. $16 \times 16 = \square$

   $15 \times 17 = \square$

5. $31 \times 31 = \square$

   $30 \times 32 = \square$

6. $25 \times 25 = \square$

   $24 \times 26 = \square$

7. $27 \times 27 = \square$

   $26 \times 28 = \square$

8. $42 \times 42 = \square$

   $41 \times 43 = \square$

9. $36 \times 36 = \square$

   $35 \times 37 = \square$

10. $53 \times 53 = \square$

    $52 \times 54 = \square$

Measurement

Write the equivalent measure.

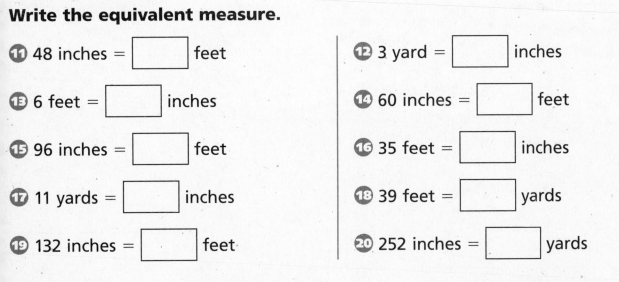

11. 48 inches = ☐ feet
12. 3 yard = ☐ inches
13. 6 feet = ☐ inches
14. 60 inches = ☐ feet
15. 96 inches = ☐ feet
16. 35 feet = ☐ inches
17. 11 yards = ☐ inches
18. 39 feet = ☐ yards
19. 132 inches = ☐ feet
20. 252 inches = ☐ yards